THE ULTIMATE INSTANT POT® COOKBOOK

THE AUSTRALIAN
Women's Weekly

THE ULTIMATE INSTANT POT® COOKBOOK

CONTENTS

ONE APPLIANCE, 9 FUNCTIONS

A multicooker appliance that can be used across a broad range of cooking applications, and combines many kitchen appliances into the one space-saving machine, is every cook's dream. While a multicooker won't shop for you or chop ingredients, it will streamline the cooking process for a variety of cooking functions. Less hands-on cooking and less washing-up throughout the cooking process are the rewards when using a multicooker. All this time saved means you'll be getting delicious meals on the table a lot more quickly.

There are an assortment of Instant Pot® models for sale in the marketplace. For this book, we used the 8-litre Instant Pot® Duo Crisp + Air Fryer when testing our recipes. Before using, read the safety and operating instructions for your specific model.

GENERAL SAFETY

Carefully read your appliance's operating manual. Failure to adhere to the safety instructions may result in serious injury. Take care with children and pets around your appliance and treat it like you would an oven or stovetop.

To avoid electric shock, it is important that you are aware that the base of the appliance and the air fryer lid contain electrical componentry that should not come into contact with water or other liquids; they should be wiped down rather than rinsed. The appliance should not be placed directly on a heat source.

PRESSURE COOKING SAFETY Before using this function, consult your appliance's manual for all safety checks required. Never use this mode without the inner pot containing liquid. Ensure that the correct lid is used, the lid is locked and valves are correctly positioned.

Never open or move the appliance while the float valve is up; wait until the pressure has completely dropped.

Do not fill the appliance's inner pot more than two-thirds full (as indicated on the pot), and no more than half full of food that will expand during cooking, such as rice or pasta.

Take care to protect yourself when releasing the pressure. Do not touch the quick release valve directly with your hands; instead, use the end of a wooden spoon.

To avoid scalding, ensure that your face and body are positioned away from the appliance when steam is released either naturally or with the quick release method, and when removing the lid.

AIR FRYER COOKING SAFETY When using this function, ensure that there is sufficient air flow around the base of the appliance, and do not obstruct the vents of the air fryer lid. Do not overfill the air fryer basket.

CLEANING

Cool the appliance before cleaning and follow the manufacturer's instructions, for safety and to preserve the life of your appliance.

COOKING FUNCTIONS

SAUTÉ Use this function with the inner pot and without a lid to sauté, sear, stir-fry and reduce, same as you would in a pan. Select the low or high setting, and once the temperature is reached, the appliance will register 'hot'.

DEHYDRATE This function uses the principles of the air fryer to create fast circulating air but at much lower temperatures, so foods dehydrate over a long cooking time. Ingredients can be placed in the air fryer basket, using either the steamer rack with handles or the perforated tray, and sealed with the air fryer lid. We recommend purchasing a 5-tier dehydrator rack to get the best use of available space.

RICE The model we used did not have a preset for rice; however, this doesn't mean you can't cook rice. Just use the pressure cooker function and lid. On average, use a 1:1 cup water to rice, for white or brown rice.

AIR FRY Use this function to circulate air around food for a crisp result using less oil. Depending on the recipe, use either the inner pot or air fryer basket with the air fryer lid. The appliance will display 'turn food' halfway through cooking. After turning, cooking will resume once the lid is replaced.

STEAM This functions the same as pressure cook, as it steams under pressure. Use this mode with the inner pot, steam rack with handles and pressure cooker lid for vegetables, chicken and fish, ensuring at least 1 cup of liquid is in the inner pot. Use the quick release method to depressurise. Once time is reached, the appliance automatically defaults to 'keep warm'.

PRESSURE COOK This function uses steam pressure to raise the boiling point of water for fast cooking. The inner pot and pressure cooker lid are required. The position of the float valve indicates pressure level. The appliance is pressurised once the valve has popped above lid level and depressurised when it has fallen. This function has three stages: coming up to pressure, cooking, and depressurisation. During depressurisation food continues to cook. There are two ways to steam release: natural release and quick release. When the quick release button has popped up, the appliance will 'naturally' release steam over time. To quick release, the valve must be turned manually.

ROAST This function is the same as air fry, with a prompt to turn food halfway through cooking. Use either the air fryer basket, inner pot or ovenproof cookware in the inner pot, with air fryer lid.

SLOW COOK Use this function to transform tough cheap cuts of meat into delicious melt-in-the-mouth dinners. Use with the inner pot and pressure cooker lid. Temperature displays as either low or high. Once cooking time is reached, the appliance automatically defaults to 'keep warm'.

BAKE This function is similar to air fry. Use either the air fry basket or place a cake pan on the steam rack in the inner pot, with the air fryer lid. The temperature can be manually adjusted, so you can bake everything from roasts to cakes and other baked goods. For even cooking, allow 2.5cm space around the cookware.

GET A HANDLE ON YOUR INSTANT POT®
CLEAR THE CLUTTER FROM YOUR BENCH WITH ONE APPLIANCE.
NEXT TO NO DISHES
01
02
03
04
05
06
07
Temp
Time
Pressure Cook
Sauté
Slow Cook
Steam
Sous Vide
Air Fry
Roast
Bake
Broil
De-Hydrate
Cancel
Start
Keep Warm
PC MAX

APPLIANCE PARTS

01 AIR FRYER LID

Use with air fry, roast, bake and dehydrate cooking functions.

02 COOKER BASE + CONTROL PANEL

The cooker base must always be used with the inner pot or the air fryer basket and accessories. The control panel shows: time, temperature and pressure display for the different cooking functions.

03 STEAM RACK WITH HANDLES

A multifunctional rack that allows for air flow and stacking, with handles to assist with removal.

04 PERFORATED TRAY

Also known as dehydrating/broiling tray, it fits in the air fryer basket, creating another level on which to stack food.

05 PRESSURE COOKER LID

Use with pressure cook and slow cook functions only.

06 AIR FRYER BASKET

Use with air fry, bake and dehydrate cooking functions.

07 INNER POT

Use the inner pot to sauté, cook rice, slow cook, steam, pressure cook and bake. The pot is hot to touch. For handling and removing, wear gloves or heat protection to protect your hands. Also, take care to wear long-sleeved clothing when reaching into the inner pot to avoid burns. The pot includes fill lines for safe volume levels.

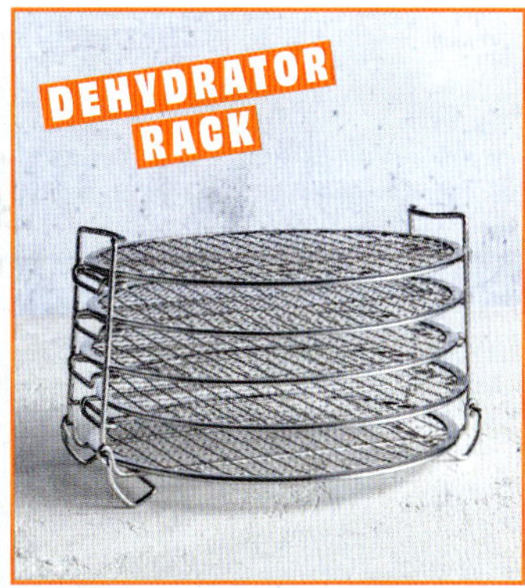

A 5-tier dehydrator rack allows you to make the most of space in the appliance, so you can dry more fruits, vegetables and meats to lock in nutrition.

CONTROL PANEL BASICS

ON Appliance is in preheat mode.

OFF Appliance is in standby mode.

LID Alert if incorrect lid is used or is not secured, or due to no lid in place.

TIME When program is in use, counts down cooking time. Time is also displayed when 'delay start' is selected and until the program begins, and displays with functions that default to 'keep warm', showing how long food has been warming.

HOT When using sauté mode and temperature is reached.

END Program is completed and does not revert to 'keep warm'.

FOOD BURN This warning can appear when food is overheating and/or when there is not enough liquid. Consult your appliance's manual for specific guidance.

SAUTÉ

DITCH THE FRYING PAN AND USE YOUR INSTANT POT®

PREP	SAUTÉ	SERVES
10 MINS	13 MINS	4

BROWN SAUCE PORK NOODLES

1 tbsp peanut or vegetable oil

3 cloves garlic, crushed

3 tsp finely grated ginger

6 green onions, sliced thinly

750g pork mince (see tip)

½ cup (140g) ground bean sauce

¼ cup (70g) oyster sauce (see tip)

½ cup (125ml) chicken stock (see tip)

400g shelf-stable fresh udon noodles

1 bunch pak choy (225g), quartered lengthways

TO SERVE
fried Asian shallots, extra sliced green onion and chilli oil

1 Select **SAUTÉ** high heat. Add oil to the inner pot. When the inner pot is hot, add garlic, ginger and green onion; **SAUTÉ**, stirring, for 1 minute or until softened. Add pork and **SAUTÉ** for a further 8 minutes, breaking mince up with a wooden spoon, until cooked through.

2 Add combined sauces and stock to the inner pot; stir until well combined. Add noodles and pak choy; **SAUTÉ** for 4 minutes until noodles are heated through and pak choy is wilted.

3 Serve noodle mixture topped with fried Asian shallots and extra green onion, drizzled with chilli oil.

TIP To make this vegetarian, use plant-based mince, vegetarian stir-fry sauce and vegetable stock.

PREP 10 MINS | SAUTÉ 19 MINS | SERVES 4

GOCHUJANG BEEF & VEGIE STIR-FRY

¼ cup (65g) gochujang (Korean chilli paste) (see tip)

2 tbsp soy sauce

2 tbsp rice vinegar

1 tbsp honey

2 x 200g sirloin steaks

1 tbsp sesame oil

2 bunches broccolini (380g), thick stems halved lengthways

200g sugar snap peas

1 tsp finely grated ginger

1 clove garlic, crushed

200g wombok (Chinese cabbage), shredded coarsely

½ cup (120g) kimchi

¼ cup (35g) roasted salted peanuts, chopped coarsely

TO SERVE
shelf-stable ramen noodles

1 Combine gochujang, soy sauce, rice vinegar and honey in a small jug. Combine steaks with ¼ cup sauce mixture and set aside.

2 Select **SAUTÉ** high heat and preheat for 5 minutes. When the inner pot is hot, add steaks and **SAUTÉ** for 5 minutes each side until browned and medium-rare (the cooking time will vary depending on the thickness of the steak). Transfer steaks to a plate, cover and rest for 8 minutes. Wipe base of inner pot with paper towel.

3 Add half the sesame oil to the inner pot, then add broccolini; **SAUTÉ** for 2 minutes. Add sugar snap peas and **SAUTÉ** for a further 3 minutes or until vegetables are tender and bright green. Transfer vegetables to a plate and cover to keep warm.

4 Add remaining sesame oil to the inner pot, then add ginger, garlic, wombok and kimchi; **SAUTÉ**, stirring frequently, for 4 minutes or until wombok is slightly wilted. Return broccolini and sugar snap peas to the inner pot with remaining sauce mixture; toss until well combined.

5 Cut steaks into thin slices. Heat ramen noodles following packet directions and serve with stir-fried vegetables and steak, scattered with peanuts.

TIP Gochujang is a spicy Korean red pepper paste available from most major supermarkets and Asian grocers.

DAIRY FREE

GLUTEN FREE
GOOD TO FREEZE

PREP 10 MINS | SAUTÉ 16 MINS | SERVES 4

ETHIOPIAN BEEF TIBS

- 600g sirloin steak, sliced thinly
- 2 tbsp berbere spice mix (see tips)
- 2½ tbsp ghee (see tips)
- 1 medium red onion (170g), sliced thinly
- 1 medium red capsicum (200g), chopped coarsely
- 1 medium green capsicum (200g), chopped coarsely
- 3 cloves garlic, chopped finely
- 4cm piece fresh ginger (25g), chopped finely
- 1 tbsp ground cumin
- 1 tsp chilli flakes
- 400g can cherry tomatoes
- 1 beef stock cube, crumbled

TO SERVE
finely chopped coriander and steamed millet

TIBS IS A POPULAR EAST AFRICAN DISH OF CUBED OR SLICED MEAT, AKIN TO A STIR-FRY. IT'S MADE FLAVOURFUL BY COOKING THE MEAT WITH CLARIFIED BUTTER (GHEE) AND A BERBERE SPICE MIX.

1 Select **SAUTÉ** high heat and preheat for 5 minutes.

2 Combine steak and 1 tbsp berbere spice mix in a medium bowl until well coated; season.

3 When the inner pot is hot, add 1 tbsp ghee. Once ghee is melted, add half the steak and **SAUTÉ**, stirring occasionally, for 3 minutes or until browned. Transfer steak to a plate. Repeat with another 1 tbsp ghee and remaining steak; transfer to plate and cover to keep warm.

4 Add remaining ghee to the inner pot. Once ghee is melted, add onion and capsicum; **SAUTÉ**, stirring, for 5 minutes or until softened. Add garlic, ginger, cumin, chilli flakes and remaining berbere spice mix; **SAUTÉ**, stirring, for a further 1 minute or until fragrant. Add tomatoes, stock cube and ½ cup (125ml) water; **SAUTÉ** for 2 minutes or until thickened slightly. Return beef and resting juices to the inner pot; **SAUTÉ**, stirring, for a further 2 minutes or until heated through.

5 Scatter beef tibs with chopped coriander and serve with steamed millet.

TIPS Berbere is an Ethiopian spice blend available from delis and specialty grocers. It can be replaced with ras el hanout or baharat spice mixes. Ghee can be replaced with butter.

PREP
20 MINS

SAUTÉ
7 MINS

MAKES
16

PRAWN SAN CHOY BAU

- **1 tbsp peanut or vegetable oil**
- **3 cloves garlic, crushed**
- **3 tsp finely grated ginger**
- **6 green onions, sliced thinly**
- **750g peeled green prawns, butterflied, deveined**
- **227g can sliced water chestnuts, drained, chopped coarsely**
- **125g snow peas, sliced**
- **2 tbsp kecap manis (sweet soy sauce)**
- **2 tbsp oyster sauce**
- **1 tsp sesame oil**
- **1 tbsp lime juice**
- **⅓ cup chopped coriander stems and leaves**
- **16 small baby cos lettuce leaves (see tip)**

TO SERVE
bean sprouts, fried noodles and roasted peanuts

1 Select **SAUTÉ** high heat. Add oil to the inner pot. When the inner pot is hot, add garlic, ginger and green onion; **SAUTÉ**, stirring, for 1 minute until softened. Add prawns and **SAUTÉ**, stirring, for a further 4 minutes or until almost cooked through.

2 Add water chestnuts, snow peas, sauces, sesame oil and lime juice to the inner pot; **SAUTÉ**, stirring, for 2 minutes or until reduced slightly and prawns are coated. Stir through half the coriander.

3 To serve, divide san choy bau mixture among lettuce leaves; top with bean sprouts, fried noodles, peanuts and remaining coriander.

TIP You will need 2 baby cos lettuces.

DAIRY FREE
PESCATARIAN

GLUTEN FREE
GOOD TO FREEZE

PREP	SAUTÉ	AIR FRY	SERVES
5 MINS	25 MINS	10 MINS	4

TARRAGON CHICKEN & GNOCCHI POT PIE

- ¼ cup (60ml) extra virgin olive oil
- 6 chicken thigh fillets (1kg), cut into 4cm pieces
- 20g butter
- 3 eschalots (75g), sliced thinly
- 2 cloves garlic, chopped finely
- ½ cup (125ml) dry white wine
- 1½ tbsp Dijon mustard
- ¾ cup (180ml) gluten-free chicken stock
- ⅔ cup (160ml) thickened cream
- 1 tbsp finely chopped tarragon
- 500g packet gluten-free baby gnocchi

TO SERVE
extra chopped tarragon

1 Select **SAUTÉ** high heat and preheat for 5 minutes.

2 Season the chicken. When the inner pot is hot, add 1 tbsp oil and half the chicken; **SAUTÉ** for 5 minutes or until browned. Transfer chicken to a plate. Repeat with another 1 tbsp oil and remaining chicken; transfer to plate.

3 Add butter, eschalot and garlic to the inner pot; **SAUTÉ**, stirring, for 3 minutes or until softened. Add wine and **SAUTÉ** for a further 2 minutes or until reduced. Add mustard, stock, cream and tarragon; stir to combine and bring to a simmer. Return chicken to the inner pot and **SAUTÉ** for 10 minutes or until chicken is just cooked through. Turn off **SAUTÉ**. Transfer mixture to a 20cm (4-cup) pie dish, ensuring the dish fits in the inner pot. Rinse the inner pot and return to the appliance.

4 Combine gnocchi and remaining oil in a medium bowl; season. Scatter gnocchi evenly over the chicken mixture. Place pie dish in the inner pot. Cover with the air fryer lid. Select **AIR FRY** and set temperature to 200°C and time for 10 minutes; **AIR FRY**, turning halfway through cooking, until gnocchi is golden.

5 Serve pot pie scattered with extra chopped tarragon.

TIP If the top of the pie looks a little dry, spray or brush with extra oil both halfway through and at the end of cooking.

PREP	AIR FRY	SAUTÉ	SERVES
10 MINS	8 MINS	16 MINS	4

MIDDLE EASTERN SPICED LAMB (LAHMACUN)

- **4 x 15cm round pitta breads (400g)**
- **1 tbsp extra virgin olive oil**
- **1 medium red onion (170g), chopped finely**
- **2 cloves garlic, crushed**
- **500g lamb mince**
- **2 tsp sumac**
- **1 tbsp baharat**
- **200g cherry roma tomatoes, halved**
- **400g can chickpeas, drained, rinsed**
- **2 tbsp finely chopped mint leaves**
- **2 tbsp pomegranate molasses**
- **⅔ cup (180g) hummus**
- **⅓ cup (50g) pine nuts, toasted**

TO SERVE
extra pomegranate molasses and extra mint leaves

1 Insert the air fryer basket with the basket base into the inner pot. Arrange pitta bread standing upright around the side of the air fryer basket. Cover with the air fryer lid. Select **AIR FRY** and set temperature to 200°C and time for 8 minutes; **AIR FRY** until pitta is crisp. Taking care, remove the air fryer basket with pitta and set aside.

2 Select **SAUTÉ** high heat. Add oil to the inner pot. When the inner pot is hot, add onion and **SAUTÉ**, stirring, for 3 minutes until softened. Add garlic and lamb; **SAUTÉ** for a further 8 minutes, breaking mince up with a wooden spoon, until cooked through. Add spices, cherry tomatoes, chickpeas, mint and molasses; **SAUTÉ** for 5 minutes. Season to taste.

3 Spread each pitta bread with 2 tbsp hummus and top with lamb mixture; drizzle with extra pomegranate molasses and scatter with pine nuts and extra mint leaves to serve.

DAIRY FREE
GOOD TO FREEZE

GOOD TO
FREEZE

PREP
10 MINS

SAUTÉ
35 MINS

SERVES
4

ONE-POT PAPPARDELLE BOLOGNESE

50g piece pancetta

1 medium onion (150g)

1 medium carrot (140g)

1 stalk celery

1½ tbsp extra virgin olive oil

500g pork and veal mince

125g tomato paste

½ cup (125ml) red wine

3 cups (750ml) chicken stock

1 sprig rosemary

500g packet fresh pappardelle

TO SERVE
finely grated parmesan

1 Finely chop the pancetta, onion, carrot and celery.

2 Select **SAUTÉ** high heat. Add oil to the inner pot. When the inner pot is hot, add pancetta and mince; **SAUTÉ** for 8 minutes, stirring frequently, breaking mince up with a wooden spoon, until browned. Add chopped vegetables and **SAUTÉ** for a further 4 minutes, stirring occasionally, until softened. Add tomato paste and **SAUTÉ** for 3 minutes or until the colour deepens. Add wine and **SAUTÉ** for a further 5 minutes until almost completely reduced. Add stock and rosemary; **SAUTÉ** until mixture boils, then cook for a further 10 minutes until slightly reduced.

3 Add pappardelle to the inner pot; pour over 1 cup (250ml) boiling water. Cover pot with foil and **SAUTÉ** for 5 minutes or until pasta is tender.

4 Serve pappardelle Bolognese sprinkled with grated parmesan.

PREP
20 MINS

SAUTÉ
16 MINS

SERVES
4

STICKY POMEGRANATE SALMON WITH EGGPLANT

½ cup (125ml) olive oil

1 large eggplant (650g), cut into 3cm cubes

1 medium red onion (170g), cut into thin wedges

2 cloves garlic, crushed

2 tbsp Moroccan spice mix

1 tsp ground cumin

1 tsp ground coriander

4 x 200g middle-cut salmon fillets, skinned, cut into 3cm cubes

¼ cup (60ml) pomegranate molasses

½ cup (140g) Greek yoghurt

1 tbsp tahini

1 tbsp lemon juice

¼ cup small flat-leaf parsley leaves

60g baby rocket leaves

TO SERVE
extra pomegranate molasses

1 Select **SAUTÉ** high heat. Add ⅓ cup (80ml) oil to the inner pot. When the inner pot is hot, add eggplant and **SAUTÉ**, stirring, for 6 minutes or until golden and softened. Add onion and garlic; **SAUTÉ**, stirring, for a further 4 minutes until softened. Add spices; **SAUTÉ** for 30 seconds. Transfer vegetables to a plate and cover to keep warm.

2 Add remaining oil to the inner pot. When oil is hot, add salmon and **SAUTÉ** for 4 minutes, turning gently, until golden. Stir through 2 tbsp molasses and **SAUTÉ** for 1 minute or until caramelised. Season to taste.

3 Combine remaining molasses with yoghurt, tahini and lemon juice in a small bowl.

4 Toss eggplant mixture, parsley and rocket together; top with salmon and drizzle with extra pomegranate molasses. Serve with tahini yoghurt.

GLUTEN FREE
PESCATARIAN

PREP	AIR FRY	SAUTÉ	SERVES
10 MINS	13 MINS	12 MINS	4

CHICKEN SCALLOPINI WITH MUSHROOMS & SPINACH

- **500g shelf-stable potato gnocchi**
- **⅓ cup (80ml) olive oil**
- **2 tbsp rosemary leaves**
- **¼ cup (20g) finely grated parmesan**
- **4 skinless chicken breasts (200g each), cut in half horizontally**
- **3 tsp coarsely chopped thyme leaves**
- **300g mixed mushrooms (see tip), sliced thickly**
- **40g butter, chopped**
- **1 tbsp lemon juice**
- **1 clove garlic, crushed**
- **½ cup coarsely chopped flat-leaf parsley**
- **100g baby spinach leaves**

1 Place gnocchi in a bowl and season. Add 1 tbsp oil, the rosemary and parmesan; toss well to combine.

2 Place the air fryer basket with the basket base into the inner pot. Add gnocchi mixture to the air fryer basket. Cover with the air fryer lid. Select **AIR FRY** and set temperature to 200°C and time for 13 minutes; **AIR FRY** until gnocchi is warmed and crisp. Taking care, remove the air fryer basket with gnocchi, cover and set aside.

3 Scatter chicken with thyme and season. Select **SAUTÉ** high heat. Add 1½ tbsp oil to the inner pot. When the inner pot is hot, add chicken and **SAUTÉ** in two batches for 2 minutes each side, or until golden and cooked through. Transfer chicken to a plate and cover to keep warm.

4 Add remaining oil to the inner pot, then add mushrooms and season; **SAUTÉ**, stirring occasionally, for 4 minutes until golden and tender. Turn off the appliance. Add butter, lemon juice, garlic, parsley and spinach to the inner pot; stir until butter melts and spinach is lightly wilted.

5 Serve chicken with mushroom mixture and gnocchi.

TIP We used a mixture of king brown, shimeji, oyster, Portobello and shiitake mushrooms.

RICE

YOUR INSTANT POT® MAKES COOKING RICE A BREEZE

PERFECTLY COOKED RICE EVERY TIME.

PREP
10 MINS

SAUTÉ
10 MINS

PRESSURE COOK
4 MINS

SERVES
4

RATATOUILLE RICE

- ⅓ cup (80ml) olive oil
- 1 medium eggplant (300g), cut into 2cm pieces
- 1 medium red onion (170g), cut into thin wedges
- 175g punnet sweet mini peppers, halved
- 2 small zucchini (180g), cut into 2cm pieces
- 4 cloves garlic, crushed
- ½ cup basil leaves, torn
- 1½ cups (300g) long grain rice
- 400g can cherry tomatoes
- 2 cups (500ml) vegetable stock

TO SERVE

goat's cheese and extra basil leaves

1 Select **SAUTÉ** high heat. Add ¼ cup (60ml) oil to the inner pot. When the inner pot is hot, add eggplant and **SAUTÉ**, stirring, for 6 minutes or until golden and softened. Transfer eggplant to a plate and cover to keep warm.

2 Add remaining oil to the inner pot, then add onion, peppers and zucchini; **SAUTÉ**, stirring, for 4 minutes until browned. Add garlic, basil and rice; stir to coat the rice. Turn off **SAUTÉ**. Stir tomatoes, stock and eggplant into the inner pot. Transfer mixture to a deep 22cm round cake pan.

3 Clean the inner pot and return to the appliance. Add 1 cup (250ml) water to the pot. Place the wire rack in the inner pot, then place the pan on top. Cover with the pressure cooker lid; lock the lid, ensuring steam release valve and quick release button are up. Select **PRESSURE COOK** low heat and set time for 4 minutes. Taking care, quick release the pressure. Stand for 10 minutes before removing the lid; this will result in perfectly cooked rice.

4 Serve ratatouille rice topped with goat's cheese and extra basil leaves.

PREP	SAUTÉ	PRESSURE COOK	SERVES
10 MINS	5 MINS	15 MINS	4

MEXICAN RICE WITH CHORIZO, POTATO & JALAPEÑO

- 3 fresh jalapeño chillies
- 1 bunch coriander
- 3 cloves garlic, crushed
- 3 tsp ground cumin
- 2 tbsp olive oil
- 2 chorizo sausages (250g), casing removed, cut into 1cm pieces (see tip)
- 1 medium red onion (170g), chopped finely
- 1 large desiree potato (400g), peeled, cut into 1cm cubes
- 2 corn cobs (800g), kernels removed
- 2 cups (400g) long grain rice, rinsed
- 400ml gluten-free chicken stock
- 100g fetta, crumbled

TO SERVE
hot sauce and lime wedges

1 Remove seeds from jalapeño chillies and finely chop. Chop three-quarters of the coriander, including the stems. Place jalapeño, chopped coriander, garlic, cumin, 1 tbsp cold water and 1 tbsp oil in a tall jug or bowl. Using a stick blender, blend to a smooth paste; season with salt.

2 Select **SAUTÉ** high heat and preheat for 5 minutes. When the inner pot is hot, add remaining oil, the chorizo and onion; **SAUTÉ**, stirring, for 4 minutes. Add potato and corn kernels; **SAUTÉ**, stirring, for a further 1 minute. Add rice and jalapeño paste; stir to coat grains. Turn off **SAUTÉ**. Add stock to the inner pot. Cover with the pressure cooker lid; lock the lid, ensuring steam release valve and quick release button are up. Select **PRESSURE COOK** low heat and set time for 15 minutes.

3 Meanwhile, chop remaining coriander.

4 Taking care, quick release the pressure. Serve rice topped with chopped coriander, fetta and hot sauce, with lime wedges on the side.

TIP To ensure this recipe is gluten free, check the ingredients list for the chorizo before purchasing and buy gluten-free chicken stock.

GLUTEN FREE

GLUTEN FREE
GOOD TO FREEZE
VEGETARIAN

PREP	SAUTÉ	PRESSURE COOK	SERVES
20 MINS	21 MINS	7 MINS	4

PUMPKIN, SAGE & GOAT'S CHEESE RISOTTO

- **1kg Kent pumpkin**
- **60g butter**
- **2 tbsp extra virgin olive oil**
- **1 large onion (200g), chopped finely**
- **4 cloves garlic, crushed**
- **1 tbsp finely chopped sage**
- **2 cups (400g) arborio rice**
- **½ cup (125ml) dry white wine**
- **1.5 litres (6 cups) gluten-free vegetable stock**
- **½ cup (40g) grated vegetarian parmesan-style cheese**
- **¼ cup (60ml) pouring cream**
- **¼ cup (60ml) lemon juice**
- **60g fresh goat's cheese, crumbled**

TO SERVE
extra finely grated vegetarian parmesan-style cheese and extra fried sage leaves

1 Cut four 125g wedges from pumpkin with the skin on; remove and discard seeds. Peel, seed and cut remaining pumpkin into 3cm pieces.

2 Select **SAUTÉ** high heat and preheat for 5 minutes. When the inner pot is hot, add butter. Once butter is melted, add the pumpkin wedges and **SAUTÉ** for 3 minutes each side or until browned. Transfer wedges to a plate. Add pumpkin pieces to the inner pot and **SAUTÉ** for 8 minutes, turning occasionally, or until golden. Using a slotted spoon, transfer pumpkin pieces to plate.

3 Add oil to the inner pot, then add onion and garlic; **SAUTÉ**, stirring, for 4 minutes until softened. Add sage and rice; **SAUTÉ**, stirring, for a further 2 minutes or until rice is slightly translucent. Add wine and **SAUTÉ** for 1 minute or until absorbed.

4 Return pumpkin pieces to the inner pot. Stir in stock and place pumpkin wedges on top. Cover with the pressure cooker lid; lock the lid, ensuring steam release valve and quick release button are up. Select **PRESSURE COOK** low heat and set time for 7 minutes.

5 Taking care, quick release the pressure. Carefully transfer pumpkin wedges to a plate. Stir parmesan, cream, lemon juice and half the goat's cheese into the risotto; season to taste.

6 Serve risotto topped with remaining goat's cheese, pumpkin wedges, extra grated parmesan and fried sage leaves.

PREP	SAUTÉ	PRESSURE COOK	SERVES
10 MINS	8 MINS	15 MINS	4

PRAWN BIBIMBAP

- ¼ cup (65g) gochujang (Korean chilli paste) (see tip on page 12)
- 2 eggs
- 2 cloves garlic, crushed
- 12 extra-large prawns (500g), peeled, deveined, butterflied
- 2 tbsp sesame oil
- 1 large carrot (300g), cut into julienne
- 2 medium zucchini (240g), cut into julienne
- 2 cups (400g) sushi rice, rinsed, drained
- 1 tbsp mirin
- 1 tbsp soy sauce
- 2 cups (160g) bean sprouts

TO SERVE
sliced green onion and white sesame seeds

1 Select **SAUTÉ** high heat and preheat for 5 minutes. Whisk 2 tsp gochujang and the eggs in a bowl. Combine 2 tsp gochujang, half the garlic and the prawns in another bowl.

2 When the inner pot is hot, add 2 tsp sesame oil. Pour in egg mixture and tilt pot to swirl mixture over base to cover; **SAUTÉ** for 2 minutes. Using a spatula, carefully flip omelette and **SAUTÉ** for 30 seconds. Transfer omelette to a plate.

3 Add 2 tsp sesame oil to the inner pot, then add prawns; **SAUTÉ**, stirring, for 3 minutes until opaque. Transfer to a plate.

4 Add 2 tsp sesame oil to the inner pot, then add carrot; **SAUTÉ**, stirring, for 1 minute or until slightly softened. Season with salt. Transfer to a plate. Repeat cooking with zucchini.

5 Add rice and remaining garlic to the inner pot; stir until grains are coated. Turn off **SAUTÉ**. Pour in 400ml water. Cover with the pressure cooker lid; lock the lid, ensuring the valve and quick release button are up. Select **PRESSURE COOK** low heat and set time for 15 minutes.

6 Meanwhile, roll up omelette; slice into thin strips. Combine remaining gochujang, the mirin and soy sauce in a bowl.

7 Taking care, quick release the pressure. Top rice with prawns, omelette strips, carrot and zucchini. Re-cover with the pressure cooker lid. Stand for 10 minutes for ingredients to warm through.

8 Serve prawn bibimbap topped with bean sprouts, green onion and sesame seeds; drizzle with the gochujang sauce mixture.

TIP Do not depressurise naturally or the rice will be overcooked.

DAIRY FREE
PESCATARIAN

GLUTEN FREE
DAIRY FREE
GOOD TO FREEZE

PREP
10 MINS

SAUTÉ
15 MINS

PRESSURE COOK
13 MINS

SERVES
4–6

CHICKEN JOLLOF RICE

8 chicken drumsticks (1.2kg)

2 tbsp olive oil

1 medium red onion (170g), sliced thinly

2 cloves garlic, crushed

1 habanero chilli, seeded, chopped finely

1 tbsp tomato paste

2 tsp curry powder

1 tbsp thyme leaves

1 cinnamon stick

2 bay leaves

400g can chopped tomatoes

2 cups (500ml) gluten-free chicken stock

2 cups (360g) basmati rice, rinsed thoroughly

300g green beans, cut into 2cm lengths

TO SERVE
lime cheeks

1 Select **SAUTÉ** high heat and preheat for 5 minutes. Season chicken.

2 When the inner pot is hot, add half the oil, then add half the chicken; **SAUTÉ**, turning occasionally, for 5 minutes or until browned. Transfer to a plate. Repeat with remaining oil and chicken; transfer to plate.

3 Add onion to the inner pot and **SAUTÉ**, stirring occasionally, for 3 minutes or until softened. Add garlic, chilli, tomato paste, curry powder, thyme, cinnamon and bay leaves; **SAUTÉ**, stirring, for a further 2 minutes or until fragrant. Add tomatoes and stock, then return chicken and any resting juices to the inner pot; season. Turn off **SAUTÉ**.

4 Cover with the pressure cooker lid; lock the lid, ensuring steam release valve and quick release button are up. Select **PRESSURE COOK** high heat and set time for 10 minutes. Taking care, quick release the pressure. Transfer chicken to a plate and cover to keep warm. Reserve cooking liquid.

5 Place rice, beans and 2½ cups (625ml) of reserved cooking liquid in the inner pot. Cover with the pressure cooker lid. Select **PRESSURE COOK** high heat and set time for 3 minutes. Naturally release for 10 minutes, then taking care, quick release the pressure. Fluff the rice and season.

6 Serve rice mixture with chicken, remaining reserved cooking liquid and lime cheeks.

PREP	PRESSURE COOK	SERVES
20 MINS	4 MINS	4

CLAYPOT CHICKEN

2 tsp sesame oil

2 tbsp oyster sauce

2 tbsp dark soy sauce

1 tbsp Shaoxing (Chinese cooking wine)

1 tbsp brown sugar

2 tbsp finely grated ginger

8 chicken thigh fillets (1.36kg), trimmed, quartered

25g dried shiitake mushrooms

1 chicken stock cube, crumbled

⅓ cup finely chopped coriander stems and roots, leaves reserved for serving

6 green onions, sliced thinly

4 star anise

2 cups (500ml) chicken stock

2 cups (400g) medium-grain rice

1 bunch gai lan (Chinese broccoli) (400g), cut into 4cm lengths

1 Combine sesame oil, sauces, Shaoxing, sugar and ginger in a bowl; add chicken and marinate for 10 minutes.

2 Meanwhile, place mushrooms in a small bowl; pour over 1 cup (250ml) boiling water and stand for 10 minutes or until softened. Remove mushrooms and finely slice; reserve soaking liquid.

3 Line base and side of the inner pot with baking paper; this will prevent food from catching on the base and the appliance turning off. Place chicken and marinade, sliced mushrooms, mushroom soaking liquid, stock cube, coriander stems and roots, green onion, star anise, stock, rice and gai lan in the inner pot. Cover with the pressure cooker lid; lock the lid, ensuring steam release valve and quick release button are up. Select **PRESSURE COOK** low heat and set time for 4 minutes. Taking care, quick release the pressure.

4 Serve chicken and rice mixture topped with reserved coriander leaves.

DAIRY FREE
GOOD TO FREEZE

SLOW COOK

DELICIOUSLY TRANSFORM TOUGH CUTS OF MEAT AND SEAFOOD

SET-AND-FORGET COOKING HAS NEVER BEEN SIMPLER.

PREP	SLOW COOK	SERVES
10 MINS	8 HRS	4–6

BEEF RIB RENDANG

185g jar rendang paste (see tips)

400ml coconut cream

2 tbsp fish sauce, or more to taste (see tips)

1.2kg beef spare ribs, cut to fit in pot

800g baby potatoes

½ cauliflower (600g), quartered

4 makrut lime leaves, stems removed, shredded finely

1 cup (230g) shredded Vietnamese pickled carrots and daikon, plus 2 tbsp pickling liquid (see tips)

TO SERVE

coconut rice (see recipe, page 78)

1 Combine rendang paste, coconut cream and 1 tbsp fish sauce in the inner pot. Add beef ribs and potatoes; mix to coat. Top with cauliflower. Cover with the pressure cooker lid. Select **SLOW COOK** low heat and set time for 8 hours; **SLOW COOK** until beef is falling off the bone.

2 Meanwhile, combine lime leaves and pickles in a bowl.

3 Stir pickling liquid and fish sauce into the curry to taste. Serve with pickles and coconut rice.

TIPS Choose a gluten-free rendang paste and fish sauce. Vietnamese pickles are available from Asian grocers.

PREP	SAUTÉ	SLOW COOK	SERVES
10 MINS	30 MINS	4 HRS	4

SPANISH-BRAISED CHICKEN & BROAD BEANS

4 chicken Marylands (1.4kg)

1 tbsp sweet paprika

¼ cup (60ml) extra virgin olive oil

200g piece pancetta, chopped finely

6 eschalots (150g), sliced thinly

3 cloves garlic, sliced thinly

1 bay leaf

500g frozen broad beans, thawed

1 cup (250ml) dry white wine

1 cup (250ml) chicken stock

TO SERVE
flat-leaf parsley leaves and toasted crusty bread

WHAT WE LOVE ABOUT THIS RECIPE IS THE HANDS-OFF APPROACH, RIGHT DOWN TO LEAVING THE BROAD BEANS IN THEIR SKINS, WHICH IN TURN BECOME MELTINGLY SOFT DURING THE COOKING PROCESS.

1 Select **SAUTÉ** high heat and preheat for 5 minutes. Place chicken and paprika in a large bowl; toss to coat. Season.

2 When the inner pot is hot, add 1 tbsp oil and half the chicken; **SAUTÉ**, turning occasionally, for 6 minutes or until golden brown. Transfer to a plate. Repeat with another 1 tbsp oil and remaining chicken; transfer to plate.

3 Add pancetta, eschalots, garlic, bay leaf and remaining oil to the inner pot; **SAUTÉ**, stirring occasionally, for 5 minutes or until eschalots are softened. Add broad beans, white wine and stock; bring to a simmer, stirring with a wooden spoon to release flavours from the base of the pot. Return chicken to the inner pot.

4 Cover with pressure cooker lid. Select **SLOW COOK** low heat and set time for 4 hours; **SLOW COOK** until chicken is tender.

5 Using a slotted spoon, transfer chicken and bean mixture to a serving dish; cover to keep warm. Select **SAUTÉ** high heat. Simmer remaining cooking liquid for 10 minutes or until reduced slightly to make a sauce.

6 Pour reduced sauce over chicken and scatter with parsley leaves. Serve with crusty bread.

TIP Chicken can also be slow cooked on high for 2 hours.

DAIRY FREE
GOOD TO FREEZE

GOOD TO
FREEZE

PREP
30 MINS (+ STANDING & REFRIGERATION)

SLOW COOK
2 HRS

SERVES
10

CHOCOLATE HAZELNUT CHEESECAKE

250g Delta Cream chocolate biscuits

80g butter, melted

500g cream cheese, softened

½ cup (110g) caster sugar

750g jar Nutella

3 eggs

2 tbsp skinless roasted hazelnuts, chopped coarsely

1 Grease a 20cm springform pan; line base and side with baking paper. Make sure the pan fits in the inner pot without touching the side; remove pan. Place the wire rack in the inner pot. Cover with the pressure cooker lid. Select **SLOW COOK** high heat and set time for 20 minutes to preheat.

2 Process biscuits to fine crumbs; add butter and process until combined. Press mixture into the base of the lined pan and smooth the surface with a spoon. Place in the freezer for 5 minutes while preparing the filling.

3 Process cream cheese and sugar in clean food processor until smooth and combined. Add 1½ cups (500g) Nutella and process until combined. With motor operating, add 1 egg at a time, processing until combined.

4 Add 1 cup (250ml) water to the inner pot. Pour filling mixture over biscuit base in pan. Taking care, place pan on the rack in the inner pot.

5 Cover the inner pot with a clean tea towel, then cover with the pressure cooker lid, wrapping the tea towel over the lid. Select **SLOW COOK** high heat and set time for 2 hours.

6 Turn off the appliance. Stand cake inside covered appliance for 1 hour. Remove the pan from the inner pot and stand for 30 minutes. Cover and refrigerate for 4 hours or until cold.

7 Just before serving, combine remaining Nutella with ⅓ cup (80ml) boiling water in a heatproof bowl; whisk until smooth. Serve cheesecake topped with the sauce and hazelnuts.

PREP	SAUTÉ	SLOW COOK	SERVES
10 MINS	9 MINS	2 HRS	4

SLOW-COOKED GINGER PORK RASHERS & CABBAGE

1 tbsp sesame oil

1kg pork rashers, halved widthways (see tips)

6 green onions, cut into 4cm lengths

1 tbsp finely grated fresh ginger

4 cloves garlic, crushed

2 tbsp gochujang (Korean chilli paste) (see tips)

2 cups (500ml) chicken stock

1 tbsp rice wine vinegar

2 tbsp soy sauce

1 tbsp caster sugar

½ small Savoy cabbage (400g), cut into 2cm wedges

TO SERVE
toasted sesame seeds, extra sliced green onion and steamed rice (optional)

1 Select **SAUTÉ** high heat and preheat for 5 minutes. When the inner pot is hot, add sesame oil, then add pork; **SAUTÉ** for 2 minutes each side or until browned. Transfer pork to a plate.

2 Add green onion, ginger, garlic and gochujang to the inner pot; **SAUTÉ**, stirring, for 1 minute. Add stock, vinegar, soy sauce and sugar; stir to combine. Return pork to the inner pot and turn to coat in the mixture. Place cabbage on top of pork. Turn off **SAUTÉ**.

3 Cover with the pressure cooker lid. Select **SLOW COOK** high heat and set time for 2 hours; **SLOW COOK** until pork is tender and falling apart.

4 Scatter pork with sesame seeds and extra green onion. Serve with rice, if using.

TIPS Pork rashers are thick-cut rasher-shaped pieces of boneless pork belly. Gochujang is a spicy Korean red pepper paste available from major supermarkets and Asian grocers.

DAIRY FREE
GOOD TO FREEZE

DAIRY FREE
GOOD TO FREEZE
GLUTEN FREE

PREP	SAUTÉ	SLOW COOK	SERVES
10 MINS	30 MINS	8 HRS	6

LAMB KLEFTIKO WITH POTATOES

- 2 tbsp extra virgin olive oil
- 1.4kg lamb shoulder (see tips)
- 1kg red and white baby potatoes, halved
- 1 large onion (200g), sliced thinly
- 2 dried bay leaves
- 1 cinnamon stick
- ⅓ cup (80ml) dry white wine
- ⅓ cup (80ml) gluten-free chicken stock
- 1 tbsp finely grated lemon rind
- 2 tbsp lemon juice
- 3 cloves garlic, crushed
- 1 tbsp rigani (see tips) or dried oregano
- ⅓ cup fresh oregano leaves

1 Select **SAUTÉ** high heat and preheat for 5 minutes. When the inner pot is hot, add half the oil, then add lamb; **SAUTÉ** for 20 minutes, turning every 5 minutes until each side is well browned. Transfer lamb to a plate.

2 Add remaining oil to the inner pot, then add potatoes, onion, bay leaves and cinnamon; **SAUTÉ**, stirring frequently, for 10 minutes or until browned.

3 Place lamb on top of potatoes in the inner pot. Combine wine, stock, lemon rind and juice, garlic and rigani in a small jug; pour over the lamb. Cover with the pressure cooker lid. Select **SLOW COOK** low heat and set time for 8 hours; **SLOW COOK** until meat is falling off the bone.

4 Serve lamb and potatoes with the cooking liquid, scattered with fresh oregano leaves.

TIPS Ensure the lamb shoulder will fit in the inner pot. Rigani is Greek-style dried oregano. It is available from specialty food stores and delicatessens. You can use dried oregano instead.

PREP	SAUTÉ	SLOW COOK	SERVES
15 MINS	14 MINS	4 HRS	4

OCTOPUS, FENNEL & SAFFRON STEW

2 tbsp extra virgin olive oil

2 medium octopus (600g each), cleaned

2 medium fennel bulbs (1kg), trimmed, cut into 2cm wedges, fronds reserved

1 medium leek (350g), sliced thinly

4 cloves garlic, crushed

¾ cup (180ml) dry white wine

1.5 litres (6 cups) gluten-free fish stock

3 bay leaves

½ tsp loosely packed saffron threads

TO SERVE
crusty gluten-free bread

1 Select **SAUTÉ** high heat and preheat for 5 minutes. When the inner pot is hot, add 1 tbsp oil, then add octopus; **SAUTÉ** for 2 minutes each side or until browned. Transfer octopus to a plate.

2 Add remaining oil to the inner pot, then add fennel; **SAUTÉ** for 4 minutes, turning, until browned. Transfer fennel to a plate. Add leek and garlic to the inner pot; **SAUTÉ** for 1 minute. Add wine and **SAUTÉ** for a further 5 minutes or until reduced. Add stock, bay leaves and saffron, then return octopus and fennel to the inner pot. Turn off **SAUTÉ**.

3 Cover with the pressure cooker lid. Select **SLOW COOK** low heat and set time for 4 hours; **SLOW COOK** until octopus is very tender.

4 Cut octopus into quarters and serve with the cooking liquid and crusty bread. Scatter with reserved fennel fronds.

DAIRY FREE
GLUTEN FREE
PESCATARIAN

PREP
10 MINS

SLOW COOK
4 HRS

SERVES
4–6

RASPBERRY & WHITE CHOCOLATE WAFFLE PUDDING

- 20g butter, melted
- 3 eggs
- 2 egg yolks
- 1 cup (250ml) milk
- 225ml thickened cream
- 1½ tbsp caster sugar
- 3 tsp finely grated lemon rind
- 1½ tsp vanilla bean paste
- 400g mini round waffles
- 2 cups (300g) frozen raspberries
- 100g white chocolate, broken into chunks

TO SERVE

- vanilla ice-cream

1 Grease a 19cm (6-cup) round baking dish with melted butter. Add 1½ cups (375ml) water to the inner pot. Fold two lengths of foil into long strips and cross under the base of the dish to act as a sling. Using the sling, lower the dish into the inner pot.

2 To make the custard mixture, whisk eggs, egg yolks, milk, cream, sugar, lemon rind and vanilla bean paste in a large jug until combined.

3 Layer a third of the waffles, raspberries and chocolate in the dish. Repeat layering twice more. Pour over custard mixture, then gently press waffles into the mixture.

4 Cover with the pressure cooker lid. Select **SLOW COOK** low heat and set time for 4 hours; **SLOW COOK** until custard is just set.

5 Using the sling, remove the dish from the inner pot. Serve pudding with ice-cream.

PREP 10 MINS | **SAUTÉ** 20 MINS | **SLOW COOK** 8 HRS | **SERVES** 4

LAMB SHANKS WITH TOMATO, FENNEL & CHILLI

- **¼ cup (35g) plain flour or rice flour (see tips)**
- **2 tbsp olive oil**
- **4 French-trimmed lamb shanks (800g)**
- **1 medium onion (150g), sliced thinly**
- **2 small fennel bulbs (400g), sliced into thin wedges**
- **1 medium carrot (120g), chopped finely**
- **2 cloves garlic, crushed**
- **1 long red chilli, sliced thinly**
- **½ cup (125ml) dry white wine**
- **410g can tomato puree**
- **400g can butter beans, drained, rinsed**
- **¼ cup chopped flat-leaf parsley**

1 Place flour in a large bowl and season.

2 Select **SAUTÉ** high heat and preheat for 5 minutes. When the inner pot is hot, add half the oil. Coat lamb in flour and shake off excess. **SAUTÉ** lamb in batches, turning, for 15 minutes or until well browned. Transfer lamb to a plate.

3 Add remaining oil to the inner pot, then add onion, fennel, carrot, garlic and chilli; **SAUTÉ,** stirring, for 5 minutes or until vegetables soften.

4 Add wine and tomato puree to the inner pot; stir to combine. Return lamb to the pot. Cover with the pressure cooker lid. Select **SLOW COOK** low heat and set time for 8 hours; **SLOW COOK** until meat is tender and falling off the bone. Stir through beans to heat through.

5 Serve lamb shanks scattered with parsley.

TIPS For a gluten-free diet, use rice flour. Serve the shanks with mashed potato, cooked pasta or sautéed cavolo nero. Suitable to freeze at the end of step 4.

GLUTEN FREE
DAIRY FREE
GOOD TO FREEZE

PESCATARIAN

PREP	SAUTÉ	SLOW COOK	SERVES
10 MINS	13 MINS	4 HRS	4

OLIVE OIL-BRAISED MEDITERRANEAN VEG

45g can anchovies in olive oil

½ cup (125ml) extra virgin olive oil

1 large onion (200g), sliced thinly

6 cloves garlic, bruised, peeled

400g green beans, trimmed

2 medium red capsicums (400g), chopped coarsely

⅓ cup firmly packed oregano leaves

½ cup firmly packed flat-leaf parsley, chopped coarsely

600g small or kipfler potatoes, peeled, cut into 5cm pieces

2 x 400g cans crushed tomatoes

1 tsp caster sugar

180g fetta, crumbled

TO SERVE
extra flat-leaf parsley leaves, extra virgin olive oil and sourdough bread

1 Select **SAUTÉ** high heat and preheat for 5 minutes. Drain anchovies and coarsely chop; reserve the oil.

2 When the inner pot is hot, add reserved anchovy oil, the olive oil and onion; **SAUTÉ**, stirring occasionally, for 5 minutes or until onion is softened slightly.

3 Add garlic, green beans and capsicum to the inner pot; **SAUTÉ**, stirring occasionally, for 5 minutes or until softened. Add anchovies, oregano and parsley; **SAUTÉ**, stirring, for a further 1 minute or until fragrant. Add potato, tomatoes and sugar, then season; bring to a simmer. Turn off **SAUTÉ**.

4 Cover with the pressure cooker lid. Select **SLOW COOK** low heat and set time for 4 hours; **SLOW COOK** until vegetables are tender.

5 Top braised vegetables with fetta and extra parsley leaves; drizzle with extra olive oil. Serve with sourdough.

TIPS Omit the anchovies to make this dish vegetarian, and replace the fetta with vegan fetta for a vegan version. Braised vegetables can also be cooked on high for 2 hours.

PREP 10 MINS | SAUTÉ 16 MINS | SLOW COOK 8 HRS | SERVES 6

MASSAMAN BEEF CURRY

2 tbsp peanut oil

2 large onions (400g), cut into thin wedges

1kg gravy beef, cut into 5cm pieces (see tip)

⅔ cup (200g) gluten-free massaman curry paste

2 x 400ml cans coconut cream

6 cardamom pods, bruised

2 cinnamon sticks

4 star anise

2 bay leaves

3 large potatoes (900g), peeled, cut into 4cm pieces

½ cup (70g) roasted unsalted peanuts

2 tbsp brown sugar

2 tbsp gluten-free fish sauce

2 tbsp tamarind paste

⅓ cup coriander leaves

TO SERVE
steamed rice

1 Select **SAUTÉ** medium and preheat for 5 minutes. When the inner pot is hot, add half the oil, then add onion; **SAUTÉ**, stirring, for 10 minutes or until lightly browned. Transfer onion to a plate.

2 Select **SAUTÉ** high heat. Add remaining oil to the inner pot, then add beef; **SAUTÉ** in batches, turning, for 5 minutes or until browned. Add curry paste and **SAUTÉ**, stirring, for a further 1 minute or until fragrant.

3 Return onion to the inner pot with coconut milk, cardamom, cinnamon, star anise, bay leaves, potato and peanuts. Cover with the pressure cooker lid. Select **SLOW COOK** low heat and set time for 8 hours.

4 Stir sugar, fish sauce and tamarind into curry.

5 Top curry with coriander and serve with steamed rice.

TIP Chuck steak is also suitable for this recipe.

DAIRY FREE
GLUTEN FREE
GOOD TO FREEZE

STEAM

LOCK IN MOISTURE WHEN STEAMING CHICKEN, FISH, VEGIES AND PUDDINGS

TRY DUMPLINGS, BROTHS, BREADS AND MORE.

PREP
10 MINS (+ SOAKING)

STEAM
25 MINS

MAKES
4

STICKY TOFFEE PUDDINGS

200g fresh medjool dates, pitted, chopped

1 tsp bicarbonate soda

1 tsp ground cinnamon

125g salted butter, melted, plus extra for greasing

1 tsp vanilla extract

2 eggs

1¼ cups (275g) firmly packed brown sugar

300ml pouring cream

½ cup (50g) hazelnut meal

1 cup (150g) self-raising flour

TO SERVE
whipped cream or clotted cream (optional)

1 Place dates, bicarb soda and ½ tsp cinnamon in a medium heatproof bowl; pour over 150ml boiling water. Cover and stand for 30 minutes to soak.

2 Meanwhile, grease four 250ml metal pudding moulds.

3 Break dates up with a fork, then stir in 75g melted butter and the vanilla. Whisk in eggs, ½ cup sugar and 2 tbsp cream until well combined. Season with a pinch of salt. Fold in the hazelnut meal and flour until just combined. Divide mixture among moulds. Cover each with a disc of baking paper then foil, pressing firmly into the side of the mould. Add 2 cups (500ml) water to the inner pot. Lower moulds into the pot.

4 Cover with the pressure cooker lid; lock the lid, ensuring steam release valve and quick release button are up. Select **STEAM** high heat and set time for 25 minutes.

5 Meanwhile, to make the caramel sauce, melt remaining butter and sugar over low heat in a heavy-based saucepan. Stir occasionally for 5 minutes until sugar is dissolved and mixture is bubbly. Stir in the remaining cinnamon and cream. Increase heat to medium and simmer for 5 minutes or until slightly thickened.

6 Taking care, quick release the pressure. Remove puddings from the inner pot and invert into bowls. Serve warm with the caramel sauce and whipped or clotted cream, if using.

TIP You could also make six puddings by using 200ml metal pudding moulds, or one large pudding using a 1.5-litre pudding bowl, and steaming for 32 minutes.

PREP
10 MINS

STEAM
2 MINS

SERVES
4

STEAMED SALMON & CABBAGE WITH ASIAN BROTH

- 2 cups (500ml) fish stock
- 5cm piece ginger, peeled, sliced thinly
- 1 cinnamon stick
- 2 tbsp yakitori marinade
- 2 tbsp Shaoxing (Chinese cooking wine)
- 100g fresh shiitake mushrooms, halved if large
- 6 green onions, cut into 4cm lengths
- ½ small Savoy cabbage (400g), cut into 3cm wedges
- 4 x 200g salmon fillets, skinned
- 200g packet shelled baby edamame (soy beans)
- 1 tbsp sesame seeds
- 1 tsp sesame oil
- 3 red radishes, cut into matchsticks
- 2 tbsp pickled ginger

1 Place stock, ginger, cinnamon, yakitori, Shaoxing, mushrooms and green onion in the inner pot. Arrange cabbage in a single layer in the pot. Place the wire rack on top of the cabbage, then place salmon in a single layer on top. Cover with the pressure cooker lid; lock the lid, ensuring steam release valve and quick release button are up. Select **STEAM** high heat and set time for 2 minutes.

2 Taking care, quick release the pressure. Gently remove salmon and cabbage from the inner pot. Strain cooking liquid into a jug, then pour ½ cup (125ml) into each serving bowl. Divide cabbage, salmon and edamame among bowls. Combine sesame seeds, sesame oil, radishes and pickled ginger in a small bowl. Serve broth topped with sesame radish mixture.

DAIRY FREE
PESCATARIAN

DAIRY
FREE

PREP
20 MINS

STEAM
4 MINS

SERVES
4

BANG BANG CHICKEN SALAD

4 green onions

½ cup (125ml) chicken stock

4 star anise

2 tsp Sichuan peppercorns

20g dried shiitake mushrooms

2 large chicken breast fillets (500g)

2 tsp sesame oil

1 tbsp black (Chinkiang) vinegar (see tip)

1 tbsp soy sauce

1 tsp caster sugar

1 tbsp peanut oil

50g snow pea tendrils

100g snow peas, blanched, shredded

4 baby cucumbers, seeds removed, chopped coarsely

¼ cup (35g) roasted unsalted peanuts, chopped coarsely

TO SERVE
chilli oil

THIS SICHUAN DISH GETS ITS NAME FROM THE SOUND OF A MEAT MALLET POUNDING THE CHICKEN TO SHRED IT AFTER COOKING.

1 Coarsely chop 3 green onions and place in the inner pot with stock, star anise, Sichuan peppercorns and mushrooms. Place the wire rack in the inner pot, then place chicken in a single layer on top. Cover with the pressure cooker lid; lock the lid, ensuring steam release valve and quick release button are up. Select **STEAM** high heat and set time for 4 minutes.

2 Taking care, quick release the pressure. Transfer chicken to a plate to cool. Strain cooking liquid into a small jug; remove the mushrooms and cool slightly. Add sesame oil, vinegar, soy sauce, sugar and oil to the jug; whisk until combined.

3 Shred chicken and place in a large bowl. Thinly slice the mushrooms and remaining green onion; add to the chicken with snow pea tendrils, shredded snow peas and cucumber. Pour over dressing and toss to combine. Serve chicken salad scattered with peanuts and drizzled with chilli oil.

TIP Chinkiang Chinese black vinegar is made from glutinous rice and has a malty sweet flavour. It is available from Asian grocers and major supermarkets.

PREP	SAUTÉ	STEAM	SERVES
10 MINS	3 MINS	6 MINS	4

STEAMED EGGPLANT WITH BLACK VINEGAR DRESSING

3 tsp sesame oil

2 cloves garlic, crushed

5cm piece fresh ginger (35g), cut into julienne

1 tsp freshly ground pepper

¼ cup (60ml) black (Chinkiang) vinegar (see tips)

1½ tbsp caster sugar

1½ tbsp soy sauce

6 Japanese eggplants (600g), halved lengthways

1 long red chilli, cut into matchsticks

1½ tbsp white sesame seeds, toasted

TO SERVE
coriander leaves

1 To make the dressing, select **SAUTÉ** high heat and preheat for 5 minutes. When the inner pot is hot, add sesame oil, garlic, ginger and pepper; **SAUTÉ**, stirring, for 2 minutes or until fragrant. Add vinegar, sugar, soy sauce and ¼ cup (60ml) water; **SAUTÉ**, stirring, for a further 1 minute or until sugar dissolves. Transfer dressing to a small jug.

2 Add 1 cup (250ml) water to the inner pot. Place the wire rack in the pot, then place eggplant in a single layer on top. Cover with the pressure cooker lid; lock the lid, ensuring steam release valve and quick release button are up. Select **STEAM** high heat and set time for 6 minutes.

3 Taking care, quick release the pressure. Transfer eggplant to a platter; drizzle with the black vinegar dressing and scatter with chilli, sesame seeds and coriander leaves. Serve hot or at room temperature.

TIPS Chinkiang Chinese black vinegar is made from glutinous rice and has a malty sweet flavour. It is available from Asian grocers and major supermarkets. Do not depressurise naturally or leave the eggplant in the appliance, or it will be overcooked.

DAIRY FREE
VEGETARIAN

VEGETARIAN
DAIRY FREE
GOOD TO FREEZE

PREP	SAUTÉ	STEAM	MAKES
15 MINS	5 MINS	3 MINS	24

STEAMED VEGIE DUMPLINGS

- 200g baby spinach leaves
- 1 tbsp vegetable oil
- 200g oyster mushrooms (or shiitake or a mixture; discard shiitake stems), chopped
- 1½ tsp finely grated ginger
- 1 bunch garlic chives, cut into 2cm lengths
- 2 green onions, chopped finely
- 2 tbsp vegetarian oyster sauce or stir-fry sauce
- 24 round dumpling or gyoza wrappers

TO SERVE
crispy chilli oil (see tips)

1 Place spinach in a heatproof bowl and pour over enough boiling water to cover. Stand for 30 seconds or until spinach wilts. Drain, then squeeze out excess liquid.

2 Select **SAUTÉ** high heat and preheat for 5 minutes. When the inner pot is hot, add oil, then add mushrooms; **SAUTÉ**, stirring, for 4 minutes. Add ginger, garlic chives and green onion; **SAUTÉ** for a further 1 minute. Stir in sauce and spinach. Turn off the appliance. Transfer spinach mixture to a bowl and leave to cool. Wash the inner pot and return to the appliance.

3 Working in batches, place 3 tsp filling in the centre of each wrapper. Using your fingertips, moisten the edge of each wrapper with a little water. Fold in half, then pinch the middle and make four pleats on each side. Repeat with remaining wrappers and filling to make 24 dumplings in total.

4 Fill the inner pot with ¾ cup (180ml) water and insert the air fryer basket. Layer half the dumplings over the base of the basket, then place the perforated tray on top. Place remaining dumplings in a single layer on the tray. Cover with the pressure cooker lid; lock the lid, ensuring steam release valve and quick release button are up. Select **STEAM** high heat and set time for 3 minutes.

5 Taking care, quick release the pressure. Arrange dumplings on a platter and serve with crispy chilli oil.

TIPS Crispy chilli oil is available from select supermarkets and Asian grocers. Do not depressurise naturally or leave the dumplings in the appliance, or they will overcook.

PREP	STEAM	ROAST	SERVES
15 MINS	50 MINS	10 MINS	8

SMOKED CHEDDAR SODA BREAD

1½ cups (240g) wholemeal self-raising flour

2 cups (300g) white spelt flour

1½ tsp bicarbonate of soda

1 tsp sea salt flakes

80g butter, chopped finely

2 cups (240g) coarsely grated smoked cheddar

1½ cups (375ml) buttermilk, approx., plus extra for brushing

½ cup (75g) mixed seeds (see tips)

cooking oil spray

CHILLI BUTTER

125g butter, softened

125g sriracha mayonnaise

1 Grease a deep 20cm round cake pan; line base and side with baking paper.

2 Sift flours, bicarb soda and salt into a large bowl. Add husks to bowl. Using fingertips, rub in butter, then stir in cheddar. Add enough buttermilk to mix to a dough. Knead dough gently on a floured surface until just smooth. Shape into a 17cm round and flatten the top. Sprinkle a third of the seeds in the base of the pan, then place dough round in pan. Brush top with extra buttermilk and sprinkle with remaining seeds. Make a shallow criss-cross cut on top of the dough. Cover pan with foil, securing with string. Make a handle with extra string.

3 Add 2 cups (500ml) water to the inner pot, then place the wire rack in the pot. Place pan on top of rack. Cover with the pressure cooker lid; lock the lid, ensuring steam release valve and quick release button are up. Select **STEAM** high heat and set time for 50 minutes.

4 Taking care, quick release the pressure. Remove pan and rack from the inner pot. Transfer bread, top-side up, to rack and spray all over with cooking oil. Place the bread on rack back in inner pot. Cover with the air fryer lid. Select **ROAST** and set temperature to 180°C and time for 10 minutes; **ROAST** until bread is golden.

5 To make the chilli butter, beat butter and mayonnaise with an electric mixer until light and fluffy. Serve warm slices of bread with chilli butter.

TIPS We used ⅓ cup toasted sesame seeds and 1 tbsp each poppy, cumin, fennel seeds and flaked sea salt. Bread will keep for 3 days or can be frozen for up to 1 month.

GOOD TO FREEZE
VEGETARIAN

PRESSURE COOK

USE THIS FUNCTION TO SPEED-COOK YOUR WAY TO FAB FLAVOURS

TRY RAGÙS, SOUPS AND, SURPRISINGLY, CUSTARD!

PREP	SAUTÉ	PRESSURE COOK	SERVES
10 MINS	20 MINS	20 MINS	6

SAUSAGE & BEEF RAGÙ

500g Italian-style pork sausages

2 tbsp extra virgin olive oil

500g lean beef mince

3 cloves garlic, crushed

1 medium onion (150g), chopped finely

1 medium carrot (120g), chopped finely

1 celery stalk (150g), chopped finely

⅓ cup (95g) tomato paste

2 tsp dried Italian herbs

⅓ cup (80ml) red wine (optional)

⅔ cup (160ml) beef stock

2 x 400g cans diced tomatoes

2 bay leaves

¼ cup finely chopped flat-leaf parsley

TO SERVE
pasta and finely grated parmesan

1 Squeeze the sausage meat from the casings and roll into walnut-sized meatballs.

2 Select **SAUTÉ** high heat and preheat for 5 minutes. When the inner pot is hot, add half the oil, then add the beef; **SAUTÉ** for 8 minutes, breaking mince up with a wooden spoon, until browned. Using a slotted spoon, transfer beef to a plate. Add remaining oil to the inner pot, then add the meatballs; **SAUTÉ** for 2 minutes, stirring, until browned. Using a slotted spoon, transfer meatballs to plate.

3 Add garlic, onion, carrot and celery to the inner pot; **SAUTÉ**, stirring, for 8 minutes. Add tomato paste; **SAUTÉ** for a further 2 minutes. Return beef and meatballs to the inner pot. Stir in dried herbs and wine; bring to the boil.

4 Add stock, tomatoes and bay leaves to the inner pot; stir well. Cover with the pressure cooker lid; lock the lid, ensuring steam release valve and quick release button are up. Select **PRESSURE COOK** low heat and set time for 20 minutes.

5 Taking care, quick release the pressure. Stir parsley into ragù. Serve ragù with your favourite pasta, sprinkled with grated parmesan.

PREP	PRESSURE COOK	SAUTÉ	MAKES
15 MINS	1 HR	40 MINS	8

MEXICAN SLOW-COOKED PULLED PORK (CARNITAS)

2.5kg boneless pork shoulder, halved, skin removed

1 tbsp ground cumin

1 tbsp ground coriander

3 tsp fine sea salt

2 tsp dried Greek oregano

1 cup (250ml) orange juice

1 cup (250ml) chicken stock

2 medium red onions (340g), sliced thinly

1 jalapeño chilli, chopped finely

½ cup finely chopped coriander roots and stems

4 cloves garlic, crushed

1 cinnamon stick

2 tbsp olive oil

8 flour tortillas (384g)

TO SERVE
sour cream, sliced pickled jalapeños, hot sauce, chopped coriander leaves and lime wedges

1 Pat pork dry with paper towel. Rub the outside with combined spices, salt and oregano.

2 Place orange juice, stock, onion, chilli, coriander roots and stems, garlic and cinnamon in the inner pot; place pork on top. Cover with the pressure cooker lid; lock the lid, ensuring steam release valve and quick release button are up. Select **PRESSURE COOK** high heat and set time for 1 hour.

3 Naturally release the pressure; this will take about 5 minutes. Transfer pork to a bowl and cover to keep warm.

4 Select **SAUTÉ** high heat and set time for 30 minutes; **SAUTÉ**, stirring occasionally, until sauce is reduced and thickened. Transfer sauce to a jug. Wipe the inner pot clean.

5 Shred pork using two forks. Select **SAUTÉ** high heat. Add oil to the inner pot, then add shredded meat; **SAUTÉ** for 10 minutes, stirring frequently, until meat is crisped. Add 2 cups (500ml) reduced sauce to the inner pot and stir to coat the meat.

6 Warm tortillas in a frying pan or wrap in foil and warm in the oven. Spoon sour cream onto tortillas, then top with pulled pork, pickled jalapeños, hot sauce and coriander leaves. Serve with lime wedges.

GOOD TO
FREEZE

GLUTEN FREE
DAIRY FREE
GOOD TO FREEZE

PREP	SAUTÉ	PRESSURE COOK	SERVES
20 MINS	22 MINS	35 MINS	4

BEEF ROGAN JOSH WITH CAULIFLOWER

2 tbsp olive oil

1.5kg chuck steak, trimmed, cut into 4cm pieces

1 medium onion (150g), chopped finely

4 cloves garlic, crushed

2 tsp finely grated ginger

1 long red chilli, seeded, chopped finely

⅓ cup (100g) rogan josh curry paste (see tip)

⅓ cup (80ml) beef stock (see tip)

400ml can coconut cream

1 cinnamon stick

4 cardamom pods, bruised

500g baby (chat) potatoes

3 tsp brown sugar

1 tbsp fish sauce (see tip)

500g cauliflower, cut into florets

300g green beans, trimmed

TO SERVE
rice or gluten-free flatbread

1 Select **SAUTÉ** high heat. When the inner pot is hot, add 1 tbsp oil, then add half the beef; **SAUTÉ** for 6 minutes or until browned. Transfer beef to a plate. Repeat with remaining beef (there is no need to add extra oil); transfer to plate.

2 Add remaining oil to the inner pot, then add onion; **SAUTÉ**, stirring, for 4 minutes or until browned. Add garlic, ginger, chilli and curry paste; **SAUTÉ**, stirring, for a further 1 minute. Add stock, coconut cream, cinnamon and cardamom. Turn off **SAUTÉ**.

3 Cover with the pressure cooker lid; lock the lid, ensuring steam release valve and quick release button are up. Select **PRESSURE COOK** high heat and set time for 30 minutes.

4 Taking care, quick release the pressure. Add potatoes to the inner pot. Re-cover with the pressure cooker lid; lock the lid, ensuring steam release valve and quick release button are up. Select **PRESSURE COOK** high heat and set time for 5 minutes. Taking care, quick release the pressure.

5 Stir sugar and fish sauce into the curry, then add cauliflower and green beans. Select **SAUTÉ** high heat; **SAUTÉ**, stirring occasionally, for 5 minutes until vegetables are tender.

6 Serve curry with rice or gluten-free flatbread.

TIP Choose a gluten-free curry paste, beef stock and fish sauce.

PREP	SAUTÉ	PRESSURE COOK	SERVES
10 MINS	18 MINS	40 MINS	4

JERK LAMB SHANKS

8 lamb shanks (2.2kg)

2½ tbsp mild jerk paste

1 tbsp plain flour

2 tbsp olive oil

1 medium red onion (170g), sliced thinly

3 cloves garlic, sliced thinly

2 bay leaves

½ cup (125ml) red wine

2 cups (500ml) beef stock

400g can black beans, drained, rinsed

500g cherry tomatoes

TO SERVE
sliced coriander leaves and coconut rice (see tip)

1 Select **SAUTÉ** high heat and preheat for 5 minutes. Place lamb in a large bowl and rub with jerk paste until well coated, then toss in flour. When the inner pot is hot, add oil, then add lamb; **SAUTÉ**, turning occasionally, for 10 minutes or until lamb is browned. Transfer lamb to a plate.

2 Add onion, garlic and bay leaves to the inner pot; **SAUTÉ**, stirring, for 3 minutes or until softened slightly. Add red wine and stock. Using a wooden spoon, scrape any bits from the bottom of the pot. Return lamb to the inner pot.

3 Cover with the pressure cooker lid; lock the lid, ensuring steam release valve and quick release button are up. Select **PRESSURE COOK** high heat and set time for 40 minutes.

4 Taking care, quick release the pressure. Transfer lamb to a plate and cover to keep warm. Add beans and tomatoes to the inner pot. Select **SAUTÉ** high heat and set cook time for 20 minutes; **SAUTÉ**, stirring occasionally, or until sauce is thickened slightly. Discard bay leaves and season to taste. Return lamb to the inner pot and stir to coat in bean mixture.

5 Top jerk lamb with coriander and serve with coconut rice.

TIP To make coconut rice, place 1½ cups (300g) jasmine rice, 1 tbsp desiccated coconut, 1 tsp salt, 1 cup (250ml) each coconut milk and water in the inner pot. Cover with the pressure cooker lid. Select **PRESSURE COOK** high heat and set time for 3 minutes. Naturally release the pressure for 10 minutes, then press quick release button down until it clicks. Allow pot to depressurise, then remove lid.

DAIRY FREE
GOOD TO FREEZE

DAIRY FREE

PREP
10 MINS

SAUTÉ
10 MINS

PRESSURE COOK
30 MINS

SERVES
4

CHICKEN PHO SOUP

- cooking oil spray
- 4 eschalots, sliced thinly
- 3cm piece ginger, peeled, sliced
- 4 cloves garlic, bruised
- 2 cinnamon sticks
- 4 star anise
- 1 tsp fennel seeds
- 1 tbsp Chinese chicken stock powder (see tips)
- 4 chicken Marylands (1.4kg)
- 1 litre (4 cups) coconut water
- ¼ cup (60ml) fish sauce, or to taste
- 200g pho dried rice noodles (see tips)
- 1 cup (80g) bean sprouts
- 2 green onions, sliced thinly
- 2 cups mixed herbs, such as coriander sprigs, Thai basil and Vietnamese mint
- 1 medium lemon (140g), cut into wedges

TO SERVE
hoisin sauce, sriracha (Thai chilli sauce) and sliced red chilli

1 Select **SAUTÉ** high heat and preheat for 5 minutes. When the inner pot is hot, spray base with cooking oil, then add eschalot, ginger, garlic, cinnamon, star anise and fennel seeds; **SAUTÉ**, stirring, for 10 minutes or until golden and well toasted.

2 Meanwhile, combine stock powder with 1 litre (4 cups) hot water in a jug.

3 Add chicken, chicken stock and coconut water to the inner pot. Cover with the pressure cooker lid; lock the lid, ensuring steam release valve and quick release button are up. Select **PRESSURE COOK** high heat and set time for 30 minutes.

4 Taking care, quick release the pressure. Using a slotted spoon, transfer chicken to a bowl. Once cool enough to handle, remove skin and bones, then shred chicken into large pieces. Keep chicken warm.

5 Drain soup into a large jug or saucepan; discard solids. Stir in fish sauce to taste.

6 Cook noodles following packet directions. Drain, then divide among bowls; top with shredded chicken, bean sprouts, green onion and herbs. Pour or ladle over the soup. Serve pho with lemon wedges, hoisin sauce, sriracha and sliced chilli.

TIPS We used Lee Kum Kee chicken stock bouillon powder. Pho noodles are flat wide rice noodles. Do not depressurise naturally or the chicken will be overcooked.

PREP	SAUTÉ	PRESSURE COOK	MAKES
10 MINS (+ STANDING & REFRIGERATION)	2 MINS	15 MINS	4

CRÈME CATALANA WITH CHERRIES

- 1½ cups (375ml) thickened cream
- ¾ cup (180ml) milk
- 4 strips lemon rind
- 4 strips orange rind
- 1 cinnamon stick
- 1 tsp vanilla bean paste
- ⅛ tsp saffron threads
- 6 egg yolks
- ¾ cup (165g) caster sugar
- 1 tbsp cornflour (100% maize)
- 125g cherries
- ⅓ cup (75g) caster sugar, extra
- 250g raspberries

1 Place cream, milk, citrus rinds, cinnamon, vanilla and saffron in the inner pot. Select **SAUTÉ** high heat and set time to 2 minutes. Turn off **SAUTÉ**. Leave cream mixture to stand in the inner pot for 15 minutes to infuse.

2 Whisk egg yolks, sugar and cornflour in a medium bowl until pale and thickened. Strain cream mixture into a large jug. Whisking continuously, gradually pour the hot cream mixture into the bowl with the egg mixture. Skim off any bubbles that form. Divide mixture among four 200ml ramekins or ovenproof dishes; cover tightly with foil.

3 Carefully pour 1 cup (250ml) boiling water into the inner pot. Place the wire rack in the pot, then place ramekins on rack. Cover with the pressure cooker lid; lock the lid, ensuring steam release valve and quick release button are up. Select **PRESSURE COOK** low heat and set time for 15 minutes.

4 Taking care, quick release the pressure. Remove ramekins from the inner pot and place in the fridge for 4 hours to chill.

5 Just before serving, halve and pit cherries. Sprinkle 1 tbsp extra sugar over the surface of each custard. Using a blowtorch, heat sugar until melted to an even golden brown. Serve topped with cherries and raspberries.

GLUTEN FREE

DAIRY FREE
GOOD TO FREEZE

PREP	SAUTÉ	PRESSURE COOK	MAKES
15 MINS	2 MINS	45 MINS	8

CHAR SIU BEEF SLIDERS

- ⅓ cup (125g) char siu sauce
- ¼ cup (60ml) rice wine vinegar
- 2 tbsp sriracha (Thai chilli sauce)
- 1 tbsp lemongrass paste
- 1 tbsp ginger paste
- 2 cloves garlic, crushed
- 2 tsp fish sauce
- 2 tsp soy sauce
- 1 tbsp caster sugar
- 1 large onion (200g), halved, sliced
- 1kg piece beef chuck steak
- 8 slider buns (320g)
- 300g packet Asian-style coleslaw (see tips)

TO SERVE
potato chips

1 Combine char siu sauce, vinegar, sriracha, pastes, garlic, sauces and sugar in a small bowl.

2 Select **SAUTÉ** high heat and preheat for 5 minutes. When the inner pot is hot, add onion, then top with beef and pour over sauce mixture; **SAUTÉ** for 2 minutes or until mixture boils.

3 Cover with the pressure cooker lid; lock the lid, ensuring steam release valve and quick release button are up. Select **PRESSURE COOK** high heat and set time for 45 minutes.

4 Taking care, quick release the pressure. Transfer beef to a plate and shred using two forks. Return shredded meat to the inner pot and stir through sauce to coat.

5 Fill slider buns with coleslaw and char siu beef. Serve with potato chips.

TIPS To make your own coleslaw mix, combine 1 cup each shredded red and green cabbage with 2 thinly sliced green onions and ⅓ cup torn parsley leaves. Only the char siu beef is suitable to freeze.

PREP	SAUTÉ	PRESSURE COOK	SERVES
25 MINS	11 MINS	35 MINS	6

LAMB TAGINE WITH QUINCE

- 2 tbsp extra virgin olive oil
- 1.5kg boneless lamb leg, cut into 3cm pieces
- 1 medium onion (150g), chopped finely
- 4 cloves garlic, bruised, peeled
- 1 tbsp ground cumin
- 1 tbsp ground coriander
- ½ tsp ground turmeric
- 1½ cups (375ml) chicken stock
- ½ tsp saffron threads
- 1 cinnamon stick
- 1 tbsp honey
- 1 tbsp finely chopped preserved lemon rind
- 1 medium quince (400g), peeled, cored, cut into 6 thick wedges
- 2 small parsnips (240g), quartered lengthways

TO SERVE
roasted chopped pistachios, flat-leaf parsley leaves and couscous

1 Select **SAUTÉ** high heat and preheat for 5 minutes. When the inner pot is hot, add 1 tbsp oil, then add half the lamb; **SAUTÉ** for 3 minutes or until browned. Transfer lamb to a plate. Repeat with remaining lamb (there is no need to add extra oil); transfer to plate.

2 Add remaining oil to the inner pot, then add onion; **SAUTÉ** for 4 minutes or until browned. Add garlic, cumin, coriander and turmeric; **SAUTÉ** for a further 1 minute. Add stock, saffron, cinnamon, honey, preserved lemon, quince and parsnip. Return lamb to the inner pot. Turn off **SAUTÉ**.

3 Cover with the pressure cooker lid; lock the lid, ensuring steam release valve and quick release button are up. Select **PRESSURE COOK** high heat and set time for 35 minutes.

4 Naturally release the pressure; this will take about 5 minutes. Top lamb tagine with chopped pistachios and parsley leaves. Serve with couscous.

DAIRY FREE
GOOD TO FREEZE

VEGETARIAN

PREP	SAUTÉ	PRESSURE COOK	AIR FRY	SERVES
5 MINS	4 MINS	12 MINS	12 MINS	4–6

SPICED LENTIL SOUP WITH ZA'ATAR CHICKPEAS

2 tbsp extra virgin olive oil

1 large onion (200g), sliced thinly

2 cloves garlic, crushed

½ tsp ground turmeric

3 tsp ground cumin

2 cups (400g) dried red lentils, rinsed

1 medium potato (200g), peeled, chopped coarsely

2 litres (8 cups) vegetable stock

400g can chickpeas, drained, rinsed

1 tbsp za'atar

2 tbsp lemon juice

TO SERVE
Greek yoghurt, extra za'atar, extra virgin olive oil and toasted flatbread (see tips)

1 Select **SAUTÉ** high heat and preheat for 5 minutes. When the inner pot is hot, add 1 tbsp oil, then add onion; **SAUTÉ**, stirring occasionally, for 3 minutes or until softened slightly. Add garlic, turmeric and 2 tsp cumin; **SAUTÉ** for a further 1 minute or until fragrant. Add lentils, potato and stock. Turn off **SAUTÉ**.

2 Cover with the pressure cooker lid; lock the lid, ensuring steam release valve and quick release button are up. Select **PRESSURE COOK** high heat and set time for 12 minutes.

3 Meanwhile, combine chickpeas, za'atar, remaining cumin and oil in a medium bowl; season. Place half the chickpea mixture in the air fryer basket, then place the perforated tray on top. Place remaining chickpeas on the tray. Set aside.

4 Taking care, quick release the pressure. Using a hand-held or high-speed blender, puree soup until smooth. Stir in juice; season. Transfer to a heatpoof bowl and cover to keep warm.

5 Rinse the inner pot and return to the appliance. Place the air fryer basket in the inner pot. Cover with the air fryer lid. Select **AIR FRY** and set temperature to 200°C and time for 12 minutes; **AIR FRY** until chickpeas are crisp.

6 Divide soup among bowls; top with yoghurt, chickpeas and extra za'atar. Drizzle with extra olive oil. Serve with flatbread.

TIPS Soup will thicken on standing; thin with a little boiling water if needed. Flatbread can be toasted in the appliance using the air fryer function.

PREP	PRESSURE COOK	AIR FRY	SERVES
10 MINS (+ REFRIGERATION)	25 MINS	25 MINS	4

ASIAN-STYLE PORK BELLY WITH CRACKLING

800g piece boneless pork belly

2 tsp Chinese five spice powder

2½ tsp fine sea salt

2 tbsp soy sauce

2 tbsp Shaoxing (Chinese cooking wine)

2 eschalots (50g), sliced thickly

5cm piece fresh ginger (30g), sliced thinly

5 cloves garlic, bruised

2 tsp caster sugar

1 star anise

1 tsp baking powder

1 tbsp vegetable oil

1 bunch gai lan (Chinese broccoli)

TO SERVE
sliced red chilli in soy sauce

1 Place pork, skin-side down, on a chopping board and rub the flesh only with five spice. Transfer pork, skin-side up, to a plate. Refrigerate, uncovered, for 2 hours or overnight.

2 Rub 1½ tsp salt into the pork skin. Place soy sauce, Shaoxing, eschalot, ginger, garlic, sugar, star anise and 1 cup (250ml) water in the inner pot; stir to combine. Place pork, skin-side up, in the pot, ensuring the skin sits above the liquid.

3 Cover with the pressure cooker lid; lock the lid, ensuring steam release valve and quick release button are up. Select **PRESSURE COOK** high heat and set time for 25 minutes.

4 Meanwhile, combine baking powder and remaining salt.

5 Taking care, quick release the pressure. Transfer pork, skin-side up, to a chopping board; reserve cooking liquid in a small jug. Using paper towel, pat pork skin dry. Pierce skin all over with a fork; rub with baking powder mixture, then brush with oil.

6 Place the perforated tray in the air fryer basket, then place the basket in the inner pot. Place pork on the tray. Cover with the air fryer lid. Select **AIR FRY** and set temperature to 204°C and time for 25 minutes; **AIR FRY** until pork is golden and crisp.

7 Place gai lan in a bowl and pour over boiling water from the kettle. Blanch for 2 minutes, then drain.

8 Slice pork belly and serve with gai lan drizzled with warmed reserved cooking liquid, and sliced red chilli in soy sauce.

DAIRY
FREE

AIR FRY
FOR THAT FRIED TASTE AND CRISPINESS WITHOUT THE FAT
COOK ALL YOUR FAST-FOOD FAVOURITES AND MORE.

PREP	AIR FRY	SERVES
10 MINS (+ REFRIGERATION)	24 MINS	4

KARAAGE (JAPANESE 'FRIED' CHICKEN)

- **1 tsp finely grated ginger, including ginger juice**
- **2 cloves garlic, crushed**
- **1½ tbsp gluten-free soy sauce**
- **1 tbsp sake**
- **1 tbsp mirin (see tips)**
- **750g chicken thigh fillets, trimmed, cut into 4cm pieces**
- **1 cup (150g) potato starch (see tips)**
- **2 tbsp sesame seeds**
- **cooking oil spray**

TO SERVE
Kewpie (Japanese) mayonnaise, shichimi togarashi (see tips) and finely shredded cabbage salad with a sesame dressing

1 Combine ginger, garlic, soy sauce, sake and mirin in a large bowl; add chicken and mix until well coated. Cover and refrigerate for 30 minutes to marinate.

2 Meanwhile, combine potato starch and sesame seeds in a bowl. Toss drained chicken in the mixture to coat, shaking off excess. Spray chicken with cooking oil until well coated.

3 Place the air fryer basket in the inner pot. Place a quarter of the chicken, evenly spaced, in the basket, then place the perforated tray on top. Place another quarter of the chicken, evenly spaced, on the tray. Cover with the air fryer lid. Select **AIR FRY** and set temperature to 204°C and time for 12 minutes; **AIR FRY**, turning halfway through cooking, until chicken is lightly golden. Repeat with remaining chicken.

4 Serve karaage with mayonnaise sprinkled with togarashi, and cabbage salad.

TIPS Most mirin is gluten free; however, check the label first. Potato starch is available from Asian grocers and should not be confused with potato flour. Shichimi togarashi (Japanese seven spice mix) is available from major supermarkets.

PREP
10 MINS

AIR FRY
13 MINS

SERVES
4

SESAME & CHILLI BROCCOLINI WITH MUSHROOMS

2 bunches broccolini (700g), trimmed

2 long red chillies, seeded, sliced thickly

100g enoki mushrooms, trimmed, separated into clusters

150g oyster mushrooms, large ones torn

1 tbsp sesame oil

3 cloves garlic, sliced thinly

1 tbsp white sesame seeds

2 tbsp gluten-free vegetarian oyster sauce

1 Place the air fryer basket in the inner pot. Cover with the air fryer lid. Select **AIR FRY** and set temperature to 180°C and time for 3 minutes to preheat.

2 Place broccolini, chilli and mushrooms in a large bowl; add sesame oil and toss well to coat. Season.

3 Taking care, place vegetable mixture in the air fryer basket. Cover with the air fryer lid. Select **AIR FRY** and set temperature to 180°C and time for 10 minutes; **AIR FRY**, tossing halfway through cooking, until vegetables are beginning to crisp at the edges.

4 Sprinkle vegetables with garlic and sesame seeds. Cover with the air fryer lid. Select **AIR FRY** and set temperature to 180°C and time for 3 minutes; **AIR FRY** until vegetables are tender.

5 Serve vegetables drizzled with oyster sauce.

DAIRY FREE
GLUTEN FREE
VEGETARIAN

PREP 10 MINS

AIR FRY 10 MINS

SERVES 4

CARAMELISED ONION & PROSCIUTTO BURGERS

750g pork and veal mince (see tips)

1 egg, beaten lightly

½ cup (40g) finely grated parmesan

¼ cup (70g) onion relish

¼ cup (25g) sage and onion stuffing mix

8 slices prosciutto

1 baby cos lettuce, shredded

4 brioche hamburger buns, split, toasted (see tips)

4 slices mozzarella

TO SERVE

extra onion relish and oven fries (see tips)

1 Combine mince, egg, parmesan, relish and stuffing mix in a large bowl; season with salt and pepper. Shape into four patties. Wrap 2 slices prosciutto around each patty.

2 Place the air fryer basket in the inner pot. Arrange patties in a single layer in the basket. Cover with the air fryer lid. Select **AIR FRY** and set temperature to 200°C and time for 10 minutes; **AIR FRY**, turning halfway through cooking, until patties are browned and cooked through.

3 Place shredded lettuce and a patty on the base of each brioche bun; top with a slice of mozzarella and extra onion relish, then sandwich together with brioche lids. Serve burgers with fries.

TIPS Pork and veal mince is a perfect blend of flavour and fattiness. You can also use 100 per cent beef or lamb mince, but avoid chicken as it tends to be too lean. You can air fry the brioche buns for 4 minutes to toast. You can also air fry the fries following packet directions.

PREP 10 MINS | AIR FRY 28 MINS | MAKES 16

POTATO, SALMON & DILL CROQUETTES

475g ready-to-serve mashed potato

300g hot-smoked salmon, skin removed, flaked

3 green onions, sliced thinly

½ cup (60g) grated cheddar

3 eggs

1 tbsp Dijon mustard

1½ cups (150g) sage and onion stuffing mix

2 tbsp finely chopped dill (see tip)

2 tbsp finely chopped flat-leaf parsley (see tip)

olive oil spray

TO SERVE
extra dill sprigs (optional), lemon aïoli swirled with harissa paste and lemon wedges

1 Place mashed potato in a medium bowl and stir until smooth. Add salmon, green onion, cheddar, 1 egg, mustard, ½ cup (50g) stuffing mix and the dill; stir to combine. Season to taste.

2 Whisk remaining eggs in a shallow bowl. Place remaining stuffing mix and the parsley in another shallow bowl.

3 Shape potato mixture into 16 x 8cm ovals. Working with one at a time, dip in egg, then coat in stuffing and parsley mix.

4 Place the air fryer basket in the inner pot. Spray croquettes with olive oil to coat well. Arrange half the croquettes in a single layer in the air fryer basket. Cover with the air fryer lid. Select **AIR FRY** and set temperature to 204°C and time for 14 minutes; **AIR FRY**, turning halfway through cooking, until croquettes are golden. Repeat with remaining croquettes.

5 Scatter croquettes with extra dill sprigs. Serve with lemon aïoli swirled with a little harissa, and lemon wedges.

TIP You can omit the dill and double the quantity of parsley, if you prefer.

GOOD TO FREEZE
PESCATARIAN

GOOD TO
FREEZE

PREP	AIR FRY	SAUTÉ	SERVES
10 MINS (+ COOLING & REFRIGERATION)	30 MINS	8 MINS	8

LEMON & BLUEBERRY CHEESECAKE

70g unsalted butter, melted

125g digestive biscuits

750g cream cheese, at room temperature

3 eggs

395g can sweetened condensed milk

2 tsp finely grated lemon rind

½ tsp sea salt flakes

2 cups (300g) frozen blueberries, thawed

2 tbsp lemon juice

⅓ cup (75g) caster sugar

1 Grease an 18cm springform cake pan with a little of the melted butter; line base with baking paper.

2 Process biscuits to fine crumbs. Add remaining melted butter and process until combined. Press mixture over the base of the pan. Freeze for 10 minutes.

3 Meanwhile, beat cream cheese in a large bowl with an electric mixer for 2 minutes or until smooth. Add eggs one at a time, beating well after each addition. Add condensed milk, lemon rind and salt; beat for 2 minutes or until creamy and smooth. Transfer mixture to a jug.

4 Place the air fryer base in the inner pot. Lower pan into the pot. Carefully pour cheesecake mixture into the pan. Cover with the air fryer lid. Select **AIR FRY** and set temperature to 150°C and time for 30 minutes; **AIR FRY** until cheesecake is firm around the edge with a slight wobble in the centre. Remove the air fryer lid. Leave to cool in the inner pot at room temperature for 1 hour, then transfer pan to the fridge for at least 6 hours to chill.

5 Meanwhile, to make the blueberry syrup, place blueberries, lemon juice and sugar in the inner pot. Select **SAUTÉ** high heat; **SAUTÉ** for 8 minutes until syrup is thickened slightly. Transfer to a jug and refrigerate until needed.

6 Release cheesecake from the pan and transfer to a plate. Serve with blueberry syrup drizzled over the top.

TIP If you don't have a processor, crush biscuits in a sandwich bag with a rolling pin. Place in a bowl and stir in melted butter.

PREP	PRESSURE COOK	AIR FRY	SERVES
10 MINS	1 MIN	15 MINS	6

CRISP GNOCCHI WITH CREAMY PESTO DIPPING SAUCE

500g packet refrigerated ready-made potato gnocchi (see tip)

1 tbsp extra virgin olive oil

1 tsp garlic salt

CREAMY PESTO DIPPING SAUCE

½ cup firmly packed basil leaves

2 tbsp pine nuts, toasted

2 tbsp finely grated vegetarian parmesan-style cheese

1 clove garlic, crushed

⅓ cup (80g) sour cream

TO SERVE
sea salt flakes and basil leaves (optional)

1 Fill the inner pot with 1½ cups (375ml) water, then add gnocchi. Cover with the pressure cooker lid; lock the lid, ensuring steam release valve and quick release button are up. Select **PRESSURE COOK** high heat and set time for 1 minute. Naturally release the pressure for 3 minutes, then taking care, quick release the pressure; this will result in perfectly cooked gnocchi. Taking care, drain gnocchi well. Spread gnocchi over a tray to air dry. Dry the inner pot and return to the appliance. Place the air fryer basket in the inner pot.

2 To make the creamy pesto dipping sauce, process basil, pine nuts, parmesan and garlic in a small food processor until finely chopped. Add sour cream and process until smooth. Season to taste.

3 Place gnocchi, oil and garlic salt in a large bowl; toss to coat the gnocchi in oil mixture.

4 Place gnocchi in the air fryer basket. Cover with the air fryer lid. Select **AIR FRY** and set temperature to 200°C and time for 15 minutes; **AIR FRY**, stirring occasionally, until gnocchi is golden.

5 Sprinkle gnocchi with salt flakes and scatter with basil leaves. Serve with creamy pesto dipping sauce.

TIP Substitute potato gnocchi for pumpkin or beetroot gnocchi.

·VEGETARIAN·

GOOD TO
FREEZE

PREP	AIR FRY	SERVES
10 MINS	15 MINS	4

CORN CHIP-COATED CHICKEN WITH RANCH SAUCE

- 200g corn chips
- 1 tsp dried oregano
- 1 tsp smoked paprika
- 1 tsp sea salt flakes
- ½ tsp mustard powder
- ¼ cup (35g) plain flour
- 2 eggs
- 16 chicken tenderloins (1.2kg)
- olive oil cooking spray

RANCH SAUCE

- ½ cup (120g) sour cream
- ½ cup (150g) mayonnaise
- ½ cup (125ml) buttermilk
- ¼ cup finely chopped dill
- 1 green onion, sliced finely
- 1 tbsp lemon juice

1 Place corn chips in a large zip-top sandwich bag and seal. Use your hands or a rolling pin to crush the corn chips, then transfer to a shallow bowl and stir in oregano, paprika, salt flakes and mustard powder. Place flour in a second shallow bowl. Lightly beat eggs in a third shallow bowl. Dust chicken in flour mixture, shaking off excess, then dip in egg and coat in corn chips. Spray generously all over with oil.

2 Place the air fryer basket in the inner pot. Cover with the air fryer lid. Select **AIR FRY** and set temperature to 180°C and time for 3 minutes to preheat.

3 To make the ranch sauce, combine ingredients in a medium bowl. Transfer to a serving bowl.

4 Spray the air fryer basket with oil. Place half the coated chicken in the basket, then place the perforated tray on top and spray with oil. Place remaining coated chicken on the tray. Cover with the air fryer lid. Select **AIR FRY** and set temperature to 180°C and time for 15 minutes; **AIR FRY**, turning halfway through cooking, until chicken is golden and cooked through.

5 Serve corn chip-coated chicken with ranch sauce.

TIP You could also serve the chicken with mayonnaise swirled with sriracha sauce.

PREP	PRESSURE COOK	SAUTÉ	AIR FRY	SERVES
5 MINS	2 MINS	8 MINS	9 MINS	4

CHURROS SHELLS WITH CHOCOLATE SAUCE

250gm conchiglioni (large pasta shells)

125g dark chocolate, chopped

½ cup (125ml) thickened cream

olive oil cooking spray

40g butter, melted

1 tsp ground cinnamon

⅓ cup (75g) caster sugar

1 Fill the inner pot with 2 cups (500ml) water, then add the pasta. Cover with the pressure cooker lid; lock the lid, ensuring steam release valve and quick release button are up. Select **PRESSURE COOK** high heat and set time for 2 minutes. Naturally release the pressure for 3 minutes, then taking care, quick release the pressure; this will result in perfectly cooked pasta. Taking care, drain pasta well. Spread pasta over a clean tea towel to air dry. Dry the inner pot and return to the appliance.

2 Meanwhile, to make the chocolate sauce, place chocolate and cream in a small heatproof bowl, then place bowl in the inner pot. Select **SAUTÉ** low heat and set time for 8 minutes; **SAUTÉ**, stirring occasionally, until the sauce is smooth and combined. Carefully remove the bowl from the inner pot and cover to keep warm. Wash the inner pot and return to the appliance.

3 Spray the air fryer basket with oil and place in the inner pot. Place pasta in a bowl and toss with melted butter to coat. Add pasta to the air fryer basket. Cover with the air fryer lid. Select **AIR FRY** and set temperature to 200°C and time for 9 minutes; **AIR FRY**, stirring, until pasta is golden.

4 Meanwhile, to make the cinnamon sugar, combine cinnamon and sugar in a shallow bowl. Immediately place hot pasta in cinnamon sugar and toss to coat.

5 Serve churros shells with warm chocolate sauce.

DAIRY FREE
PESCATARIAN

PREP
10 MINS

AIR FRY
6 MINS

MAKES
4

SPICED GARLIC PRAWN PO'BOY

- **3 eggs**
- **1¼ cups (95g) panko (Japanese) breadcrumbs**
- **1½ tbsp Cajun seasoning**
- **24 uncooked prawns, peeled, deveined**
- **olive oil cooking spray**
- **4 long bread rolls (280g)**
- **⅓ cup (100g) mayonnaise**
- **1 baby cos lettuce (180g), shredded**
- **2 medium tomatoes (300g), sliced thinly**
- **3 gherkins, cut into rounds**

TO SERVE
extra mayonnaise, hot sauce, chopped chives, extra gherkins and chips

1 Lightly beat eggs and 1 tbsp water in a shallow bowl. Combine breadcrumbs and seasoning in a second shallow bowl. Dip prawns in egg, then coat in breadcrumb mixture. Spray generously all over with oil.

2 Place the air fryer basket in the inner pot. Cover with the air fryer lid. Select **AIR FRY** and set temperature to 180°C and time for 3 minutes to preheat.

3 Taking care, place coated prawns in a single layer in the air fryer basket. Cover with the air fryer lid. Select **AIR FRY** and set temperature to 180°C and time for 6 minutes; **AIR FRY**, turning halfway through cooking, until prawns are golden brown and cooked through.

4 Split bread rolls horizontally, being careful not to cut all the way through. Spread bases with mayonnaise, then fill with lettuce, tomatoes, prawns and gherkins. Drizzle with extra mayonnaise and hot sauce; sprinkle with chopped chives. Serve with extra gherkins and chips.

PREP
10 MINS

AIR FRY
4 MINS

SERVES
4 (AS A SNACK)

FURIKAKE ASPARAGUS

1 cup (75g) panko (Japanese) breadcrumbs

¼ cup (30g) furikake (see tip)

1 tbsp sesame oil

2 eggs

2 bunches thick asparagus (340g), trimmed

cooking oil spray

1 tsp wasabi

⅓ cup (100g) Kewpie (Japanese) mayonnaise

TO SERVE
extra furikake and lemon cheeks

1 Place breadcrumbs, furikake and sesame oil in a medium bowl; stir to combine. Transfer breadcrumb mixture to a tray. Using a fork, lightly beat eggs in a shallow bowl; season.

2 Place the air fryer basket in the inner pot. Cover with the air fryer lid. Select **AIR FRY** and set temperature to 180°C and time for 3 minutes to preheat.

3 Dip asparagus in egg, shaking off excess, then roll in breadcrumb mixture. Place on an oven tray and spray generously with oil to coat all sides.

4 Spray the air fryer basket with oil. Place half the coated asparagus in the basket, then place the perforated tray on top and spray with oil. Place remaining coated asparagus on the tray. Cover with the air fryer lid. Select **AIR FRY** and set temperature to 180°C and time for 4 minutes; **AIR FRY** until asparagus are golden.

5 Meanwhile, combine wasabi and mayonnaise in a small bowl.

6 Sprinkle asparagus with extra furikake. Serve with wasabi mayonnaise and lemon cheeks.

TIP Furikake is a Japanese rice seasoning that usually contains toasted sesame seeds, salt, nori and sugar. It may also include bonito flakes, chilli flakes, miso powder, shiitake powder and poppy seeds. We used Nori Komi Furikake from supermarkets.

DAIRY FREE
VEGETARIAN

ROAST

GOODBYE OVEN, HELLO VERSATILE INSTANT POT®

TUCK INTO CRISP-SKINNED CHICKEN, FISH AND ROASTS.

PREP	ROAST	SAUTÉ	SERVES
10 MINS	55 MINS	7 MINS	4

NYONYA CURRY ROAST CHICKEN

4 anchovies, chopped finely

185g jar gluten-free Nyonya curry paste

1.5kg free-range chicken

2 tbsp rice bran oil

800g baby (chat) potatoes

1 bunch baby carrots (400g), trimmed, peeled, halved

200g green beans, trimmed

400ml coconut milk

TO SERVE
coriander sprigs, steamed rice and lime cheeks

1 Combine anchovies and curry paste in a bowl; reserve ¼ cup for the sauce. Rub remaining paste mixture all over chicken and under the skin of the breast meat. Tuck the wings under and tie chicken legs together with kitchen string.

2 Add half the oil and the potatoes to the inner pot; toss to coat. Add chicken to the pot. Cover with the air fryer lid. Select **ROAST** and set temperature to 190°C and time for 40 minutes; **ROAST** until chicken is cooked through. Transfer to a plate, partially cover and rest for 15 minutes.

3 Meanwhile, add carrots and ¼ cup (60ml) water to the inner pot (there is no need to clean it). Cover with the air fryer lid. Select **ROAST** and set temperature to 190°C and time for 10 minutes; **ROAST** until carrots are almost tender.

4 Add green beans to the inner pot. Re-cover with the air fryer lid. Select **ROAST** and set temperature to 190°C and time for 5 minutes; **ROAST** until vegetables are tender. Using a slotted spoon, transfer vegetables to a plate and keep warm. Drain the inner pot, dry and return to the appliance.

5 To make the curry sauce, select **SAUTÉ** high heat and preheat for 5 minutes. When the inner pot is hot, add remaining oil and reserved curry paste; **SAUTÉ** for 2 minutes. Stir in coconut milk and bring to a simmer; **SAUTÉ** 5 minutes until reduced slightly.

6 Serve roast chicken with vegetables, coriander sprigs, curry sauce, rice and lime cheeks.

PREP
15 MINS (+ REFRIGERATION & RESTING)

ROAST
45 MINS

SERVES
4

CHINESE-STYLE ROAST LAMB

1 small red onion (100g), chopped coarsely

4 cloves garlic, peeled

4cm piece ginger, peeled, chopped coarsely

1 long red chilli, chopped coarsely

¾ cup coarsely chopped coriander stems, roots and leaves

1 tbsp ground cumin

1 tbsp ground coriander

½ tsp ground white pepper

2 tbsp sesame oil

2 tbsp rice wine vinegar

¼ cup (60ml) soy sauce

1.8kg boned lamb leg, trimmed, halved

TO SERVE
steamed Asian greens and steamed rice

1 Process onion, garlic, ginger, chilli, coriander, spices, pepper, sesame oil, vinegar and soy sauce until almost smooth. Place lamb in a large dish and pour over spice mixture to coat; cover and refrigerate for 3 hours or overnight.

2 Place the wire rack in the inner pot. Place lamb on the rack and pour over any marinade. Cover with the air fryer lid. Select **ROAST** and set temperature to 200°C and time for 45 minutes; **ROAST** until lamb is cooked through.

3 Remove the air fryer lid. Partially cover the lamb and rest for 10 minutes in the inner pot. Slice lamb and serve drizzled with cooking juices, with Asian greens and steamed rice.

DAIRY FREE

DAIRY FREE
PESCATARIAN
GLUTEN FREE

PREP 10 MINS | **ROAST** 39 MINS | **SERVES** 4

ONE-POT SALMON NIÇOISE BAKE

- 500g kipfler potatoes, halved lengthways
- 1 medium bulb garlic, cloves separated
- ¼ cup (60ml) extra virgin olive oil
- 4 eggs, washed
- 200g truss cherry tomatoes
- ½ cup (80g) pitted Kalamata olives
- 4 x 150g boneless salmon fillets, skin on
- 200g green beans, trimmed

SALSA VERDE

- ½ cup firmly packed flat-leaf parsley
- ½ cup firmly packed baby spinach
- 4 anchovy fillets
- 2 tbsp baby capers
- 2 tbsp lemon juice
- ½ cup (125ml) extra virgin olive oil

1 Place potatoes and garlic in the inner pot; drizzle with 1 tbsp oil; season. Place the wire rack in the inner pot, then place eggs on top. Cover with the air fryer lid. Select **ROAST** and set temperature to 200°C and time for 10 minutes; **ROAST**, stirring potatoes halfway through cooking and turning eggs.

2 Remove eggs and plunge into a bowl of ice-cold water, then peel and set aside. Re-cover with the air fryer lid. Select **ROAST** and set temperature to 200°C and time for 15 minutes; **ROAST** until potatoes and garlic are golden. Transfer potatoes and garlic to a plate and cover to keep warm.

3 Add cherry tomatoes and olives to the inner pot; drizzle with remaining oil. Cover with the air fryer lid. Select **ROAST** and set temperature to 200°C and time for 10 minutes.

4 Push tomato mixture to one side of the inner pot. Add seasoned salmon to the other side, skin side down, ensuring salmon sits directly on the base of the pot. Re-cover with the air fryer lid. Select **ROAST** and set temperature to 200°C and time for 2 minutes. Turn salmon over and add green beans; **ROAST** for a further 2 minutes at 200°C or until salmon is just cooked through and green beans are tender.

5 Meanwhile, to make the salsa verde, process ingredients in a small food processor until combined.

6 Arrange salmon, potatoes, garlic, cherry tomatoes, green beans, olives and halved eggs on a platter or plates. Serve with salsa verde.

PREP	PRESSURE COOK	SAUTÉ	ROAST	SERVES
15 MINS	1 MIN	5 MINS	1 HR	6

CHORIZO & SEMI-DRIED TOMATO TORTILLA

3 medium potatoes (600g), peeled, cut into 5mm-thick slices

2 tbsp extra virgin olive oil

1 large onion (200g), sliced thinly

2 cloves garlic, crushed

250g cured chorizo sausages, sliced thinly

¾ cup (135g) semi-dried tomatoes, chopped coarsely

2 medium zucchini (240g), grated coarsely, squeezed dry

10 eggs, beaten lightly

1 cup (120g) coarsely grated cheddar

2 cups (35g) red-vein sorrel or rocket

1 tbsp balsamic vinegar

⅓ cup (25g) shaved parmesan

1 Place potatoes and 1½ cups (375ml) water in the inner pot. Select **PRESSURE COOK** high heat and set time for 1 minute. Taking care, quick release the pressure. Drain potato slices, then spread out on a tray to cool. Dry the inner pot and return to the appliance.

2 Select **SAUTÉ** high heat and preheat for 5 minutes. Add the oil. When oil is hot, add onion, garlic and chorizo; **SAUTÉ**, stirring, for 5 minutes or until onion is soft. Stir in semi-dried tomatoes and zucchini; season to taste.

3 Grease a deep 20cm round cake pan; line base and side with baking paper. Combine egg and half the cheddar; season. Cover the base with potato slices, then pour over half the egg mixture. Spread chorizo mixture evenly over potatoes. Pour remaining egg mixture over chorizo mixture, then scatter with remaining cheddar. Cover pan with foil.

4 Place the wire rack in the inner pot, then place the pan on top. Cover with the air fryer lid. Select **ROAST** and set temperature to 200°C and time for 50 minutes.

5 Remove the foil, then re-cover with the air fryer lid. Select **ROAST** and set temperature to 200°C and time for 10 minutes; **ROAST** until top is golden.

6 Toss sorrel with remaining oil, the vinegar and parmesan; season to taste. Serve tortilla with salad.

GOOD TO
FREEZE

DAIRY
FREE

PREP
10 MINS (+ RESTING)

ROAST
30 MINS

SERVES
4

TAMARIND PORK BELLY

- 4 cloves garlic, crushed
- 2 tbsp finely grated ginger
- 6 green onions, chopped finely
- 1 long red chilli, seeded, chopped finely
- 1½ tbsp tamarind puree
- 1 tbsp roasted sesame oil
- ¼ cup (60ml) soy sauce
- 1½ tbsp fish sauce
- 2½ tbsp brown sugar
- 1kg piece pork belly, skin removed
- ½ chicken stock cube
- 1 tbsp lime juice

TO SERVE

- shredded green cabbage

1 Combine garlic, ginger, green onion, chilli, tamarind, sesame oil, soy sauce, fish sauce and sugar in a large bowl; add pork and toss to coat.

2 Remove pork from the marinade. Pour marinade into the inner pot, then crumble in stock cube. Place the wire rack in the inner pot, then place pork on top. Cover with the air fryer lid. Select **ROAST** and set temperature to 200°C and time for 30 minutes; **ROAST** until pork is tender and cooked through.

3 Remove the air fryer lid. Partially cover the pork and rest for 10 minutes in the inner pot before slicing. Stir lime juice into the sauce in the pot.

4 Serve pork drizzled with a little of the sauce, with remaining sauce and shredded cabbage on the side.

PREP	SAUTÉ	ROAST	SERVES
10 MINS	10 MINS	35 MINS	4

MISO CHICKPEA LOADED SWEET POTATOES

2 tbsp extra virgin olive oil

2 large red onions (600g), each cut into 8 wedges

4 cloves garlic, sliced thinly

2 long red chillies, halved lengthways

1 tbsp finely grated ginger

1 cup (250ml) salt-reduced vegetable stock

1½ tbsp tamari

1½ tbsp maple syrup

1 tbsp lemon juice

2½ tbsp red (aka) miso

2 x 400g cans chickpeas, drained, rinsed

4 small orange sweet potatoes (1kg)

40g butter

2 green onions, shredded

¼ cup coriander leaves

1 Select **SAUTÉ** high heat and preheat for 5 minutes. When the inner pot is hot, add oil, then add onion; **SAUTÉ**, stirring, for 5 minutes or until onion is softened. Add garlic, chilli and ginger; **SAUTÉ**, stirring, for a further 2 minutes.

2 Whisk stock, tamari, maple syrup, lemon juice and miso in a jug; add to the inner pot. Select **SAUTÉ** high heat and bring to the boil, then boil for 1 minute. Stir in chickpeas.

3 Prick sweet potatoes several times with a fork and place on top of chickpea mixture. Cover with the air fryer lid. Select **ROAST** and set temperature to 200°C and time for 35 minutes; **ROAST** until sweet potatoes are tender. Transfer sweet potatoes to plates. With a small, sharp knife, slit top of sweet potatoes lengthways to open them up.

4 Gently stir butter into chickpea mixture in the inner pot until combined.

5 Fill sweet potatoes with chickpea mixture. Serve topped with green onion and coriander.

VEGETARIAN

DAIRY FREE
VEGETARIAN

PREP
15 MINS

ROAST
40 MINS

SERVES
4

MISO-ROASTED CAULI WITH ALMOND CREAM

- 1.3kg whole cauliflower
- 2 tbsp white (shiro) miso paste (see tips)
- 2 tbsp gochujang (Korean chilli paste) (see tips)
- ¼ cup (60ml) maple syrup
- 2 tbsp extra virgin olive oil
- 1 tbsp finely grated ginger
- 2 cloves garlic, crushed
- 1 cup (250ml) Shaoxing (Chinese cooking wine)
- 1 tbsp sesame seeds

ALMOND CREAM

- 1¼ cups (200g) flaked almonds
- ¼ cup (75g) Kewpie (Japanese) mayonnaise
- 1½ tbsp white (shiro) miso paste
- 2 tbsp yuzu juice or lemon juice (see tips)

1 Cut a cross in the base of the cauliflower with a sharp knife. Combine miso, gochujang, maple syrup, oil, ginger and garlic in a small bowl; season. Spread mixture over cauliflower. Pour Shoaxing into the inner pot, then place cauliflower in the pot.

2 Cover the inner pot with foil, then cover with the air fryer lid. Select **ROAST** and set temperature to 200°C and time for 25 minutes.

3 Remove the foil, sprinkle cauliflower with sesame seeds, then re-cover with the air fryer lid. Select **ROAST** and set temperature to 200°C and time for 15 minutes; **ROAST** until cauliflower is tender and lightly browned.

4 Meanwhile, to make the almond cream, place almonds in a heatproof bowl and cover with boiling water. Stand until cooled, then drain. Blend soaked almonds with remaining ingredients and ¾ cup (180ml) water until smooth.

5 Serve roasted cauliflower with almond cream.

TIPS Shiro (white) miso is sweeter and milder in taste than brown, red and black miso. It is available from most major supermarkets and Asian grocers. Gochujang is a spicy Korean red pepper paste available from most major supermarkets and Asian grocers. Yuzu juice is available from Asian grocers.

PREP
10 MINS (+ REFRIGERATION)

ROAST
1 HR 45 MINS

SAUTÉ
7 MINS

SERVES
4

KOREAN ROAST BEEF WITH BRAISED CABBAGE

¼ cup (75g) gochujang (Korean chilli paste) (see tip)

3 cloves garlic, crushed

4cm piece fresh ginger (30g), grated finely

1 tbsp brown sugar

2 tsp sesame oil

1kg bolar blade beef

1 small wombok (700g), chopped coarsely

2 green onions, cut into 5cm lengths

2 tsp fish sauce

1 cup (250ml) beef stock

TO SERVE
steamed rice

1 Combine gochujang, garlic, ginger, sugar and sesame oil in a small bowl; reserve 1 tbsp marinade. Place beef in a large dish and rub with the marinade; cover and refrigerate for at least 4 hours or overnight.

2 Place the wire rack in the inner pot, then place beef on top. Cover with the air fryer lid. Select **ROAST** and set temperature to 193°C and time for 20 minutes; **ROAST** until beef is lightly charred.

3 Cover beef with foil, then re-cover with the air fryer lid. Select **ROAST** and set temperature to 193°C and time for 1 hour 25 minutes; **ROAST**, turning halfway through cooking, until beef is medium-rare or cooked to your liking. Transfer beef to a plate and rest for 15 minutes.

4 Meanwhile, pour beef fat from the inner pot into a small bowl and reserve. Clean the inner pot and return to the appliance. Add reserved fat to the pot, then add wombok and green onions. Select **SAUTÉ** high heat and set time for 2 minutes; **SAUTÉ** until vegetables are slightly softened. Add fish sauce, stock and reserved marinade; **SAUTÉ** for a further 5 minutes or until vegetables are tender. Season to taste.

5 Slice beef and serve with vegetables and rice.

TIP Gochujang is a spicy Korean red pepper paste available from most major supermarkets and Asian grocers.

DAIRY FREE

PREP	ROAST	SAUTÉ	SERVES
20 MINS	35 MINS	15 MINS	4

CHICKEN MARYLANDS WITH SAGE BUTTER & CAPERS

4 chicken Marylands (1.2kg), skin on

2 cups (500ml) chicken stock

1 medium lemon (140g), sliced

4 cloves garlic, bruised

2 tbsp chopped sage leaves

8 corn cobettes (425g)

SAGE BUTTER

100g butter, softened

2 cloves garlic, crushed

2 tsp finely grated lemon rind

1 tbsp finely chopped sage

1 tbsp baby capers, chopped

1 To make the sage butter, combine ingredients in a bowl.

2 Pat chicken dry with paper towel. Run a couple of fingers between the flesh and skin to separate, then spread the sage butter between flesh and skin. Season with salt.

3 Place stock, lemon, garlic, sage and corn in the inner pot. Place the wire rack in the inner pot, then place chicken in a single layer on top. Cover with the air fryer lid. Select **ROAST** and set temperature to 200°C and time for 35 minutes; **ROAST** until chicken is crisp and cooked through. Transfer chicken to a plate and partially cover to keep warm.

4 Select **SAUTÉ** high heat and set time for 15 minutes; **SAUTÉ** until cooking liquid is reduced and thickened.

5 Serve chicken and corn drizzled with reduced cooking liquid.

TIP Turn chicken halfway through cooking for even browning.

PREP
20 MINS

ROAST
1 HR 30 MINS

SERVES
4

ROAST CARDAMOM PORK WITH KIPFLER POTATOES

1.6kg pork loin, skin scored (see tips)

2 tbsp olive oil

1 tbsp fennel seeds, crushed

1 cup (250ml) chicken stock

10 cardamom pods, bruised

1kg small kipfler potatoes, scrubbed (see tips)

4 small baby red apples (65g each), cored

1 Dry the pork skin with paper towel, then rub all over with oil, fennel and salt.

2 Place stock, cardamom and potatoes in the inner pot. Place the wire rack in the inner pot, then place pork on top. Cover with the air fryer lid. Select **ROAST** and set temperature to 200°C and time for 1 hour.

3 Add apples to the inner pot, placing around the pork. Re-cover with the air fryer lid. Select **ROAST** and set temperature to 200°C and time for 30 minutes; **ROAST** until the rind crackles.

4 Remove the air fryer lid. Leave pork to rest for 10 minutes in the inner pot before slicing. Serve pork with potatoes, apples and strained cooking liquid.

TIPS Let the pork dry out, uncovered, in the fridge overnight to help the skin crackle during cooking. If the kipfler potatoes are larger than 30g each, halve lengthways before cooking.

DAIRY
FREE

DEHYDRATE

USE THE AIR FRYER LID AND DEHYDRATE FUNCTION FOR LOW-TEMP COOKING

DEHYDRATE YOUR WAY TO TASTY SNACKS AND TREATS.

PREP	DEHYDRATE	SERVES
5 MINS	9 HRS	6

SPICY DRIED MANGO

WE RECOMMEND YOU USE A 5-TIER DEHYDRATOR RACK TO MAXIMISE THE SPACE OF YOUR APPLIANCE (SEE TIP).

½ tsp chilli powder, or to taste

3 medium limes (195g), rind grated finely

¼ tsp fine salt

3 x 685g cans mango slices in juice, drained

1 Combine chilli powder, lime rind and salt in a large bowl.

2 Pat mango slices dry with paper towel, then add to bowl with chilli mix and toss to coat.

3 Arrange mango slices in a single layer on a 5-tier dehydrator rack, then place in the inner pot. Cover with the air fryer lid. Select **DEHYDRATE** and set temperature to 57°C and time for 9 hours; **DEHYDRATE** until mango is dried but still retaining a little chewiness.

4 Remove the dehydrator rack from the inner pot. Leave mango slices to cool on the rack. Store in an airtight container for up to 3 months.

TIP If you do not have a 5-tier dehydrator rack, halve the recipe and place half the mango slices in a single layer in the air fryer basket, cover with the perforated tray, then place remaining mango slices on top. Place the air fryer basket in the inner pot and continue with the recipe.

PREP 10 MINS | **DEHYDRATE** 3½–4 HRS | **MAKES** 1½–3 TBSP

CITRUS POWDERS

WE RECOMMEND YOU USE A 5-TIER DEHYDRATOR RACK TO MAXIMISE THE SPACE OF YOUR APPLIANCE (SEE TIPS).

4 medium limes (260g), each cut into 6 wedges

3 medium lemons (420g), each cut into 6 wedges

2 medium tangelos (220g), each cut into 6 wedges

1 Using a spoon, scoop the flesh from the rinds and reserve for another use. Holding a small, sharp knife horizontally, remove the white pith from each citrus wedge and discard.

2 Place citrus rinds in a single layer on a 5-tier dehydrator rack, with the lime rind on the top two tiers, then place in the inner pot. Cover with the air fryer lid. Select **DEHYDRATE** and set temperature to 57°C and time for 3½ hours; **DEHYDRATE** until lime rind is no longer flexible.

3 Remove the dehydrator rack and transfer lime rind to a plate. Return the dehydrator rack to the inner pot. Re-cover with the air fryer lid. Select **DEHYDRATE** and set temperature to 57°C and time for 30 minutes; **DEHYDRATE** until lemon and tangelo rinds are no longer flexible.

4 Remove the dehydrator rack from the inner pot. Leave citrus rinds to cool on the rack.

5 Process each citrus rind separately in a high-speed blender to a powder. Store in an airtight container for up to 3 months.

TIPS If you do not have a 5-tier dehydrator rack, make a single citrus powder type rather then all three. Place half the rind in a single layer in the air fryer basket, cover with the perforated tray, then place remaining citrus peel on the tray. Place the air fryer basket in the inner pot and continue with the recipe. Use half as much citrus powder instead of freshly grated rind in cake batters, buttercreams or mixed with sugar for dusting to add a citrus flavour.

DAIRY FREE
GLUTEN FREE
VEGETARIAN

DAIRY
FREE

PREP	DEHYDRATE	SERVES
10 MINS (+ FREEZING & REFRIGERATION)	8 HRS	8

BEEF JERKY

WE RECOMMEND YOU USE A 5-TIER DEHYDRATOR RACK TO MAXIMISE THE SPACE OF YOUR APPLIANCE (SEE TIPS).

800g flank or skirt steak

½ cup (125ml) soy sauce

½ cup (125ml) Worcestershire sauce

2 tsp freshly ground black pepper

1 tsp sea salt

1 tsp onion powder

1 tsp garlic powder

1 tsp liquid smoke (see tips)

1 Trim excess fat from steak, then place in the freezer for 30 minutes to firm up; this will make it easier to slice. Remove steak from the freezer and thinly slice against the grain into long strips.

2 Whisk remaining ingredients in a jug to combine. Place beef and marinade in a large zip-top bag; seal and shake to coat the beef. Refrigerate for 2 hours or overnight.

3 Drain meat. Arrange meat slices in a single layer on a 5-tier dehydrator rack, then place in the inner pot. Cover with the air fryer lid. Select **DEHYDRATE** and set temperature to 62°C and time for 8 hours; **DEHYDRATE** until meat is dried.

4 Remove the dehydrator rack from the inner pot. Leave meat to cool on the rack. Store in an airtight container for up to 3 months.

TIPS If you do not have a 5-tier dehydrator rack, halve the recipe and place half the beef in a single layer in the air fryer basket, cover with the perforated tray, then place remaining beef on top. Place the air fryer basket in the inner pot and continue with the recipe. Liquid smoke imparts an instant smoke flavour and aroma to food. It is available from major supermarkets and select delicatessens. Alternatively, add 2 tsp smoked paprika to the marinade.

PREP 15 MINS | **DEHYDRATE** 8 HRS | **SERVES** 4

CAULIFLOWER POPCORN

WE RECOMMEND YOU USE A 5-TIER DEHYDRATOR RACK TO MAXIMISE THE SPACE OF YOUR APPLIANCE (SEE TIP).

⅓ cup (95g) gluten-free hot sauce

¼ cup (60ml) olive oil

2 tsp garlic powder

2 tsp onion powder

1 tbsp smoked paprika

2 tsp ground cumin

1 small cauliflower (1kg), cut into 2cm even-sized florets

cooking oil spray

1 Combine hot sauce, oil, garlic powder, onion powder, paprika and cumin in a medium bowl; add cauliflower and toss to coat well.

2 Spray a 5-tier dehydrator rack with oil. Arrange cauliflower on the bottom, middle and top racks, then place in the inner pot. Cover with the air fryer lid. Select **DEHYDRATE** and set temperature to 74°C and time for 8 hours; **DEHYDRATE** until cauliflower is dried.

3 Remove the dehydrator rack from the inner pot. Leave cauliflower to cool on the rack. Store in an airtight container for up to 1 month.

TIP If you do not have a 5-tier dehydrator rack, halve the recipe and place half the cauliflower in a single layer in the air fryer basket, cover with the perforated tray, then place remaining cauliflower on top. Place the air fryer basket in the inner pot and continue with the recipe.

DAIRY FREE
GLUTEN FREE
VEGETARIAN

DAIRY FREE
GLUTEN FREE
VEGETARIAN

PREP
10 MINS

DEHYDRATE
4 HRS

SERVES
4

DEHYDRATED FRUIT

WE RECOMMEND YOU USE A 5-TIER DEHYDRATOR RACK TO MAXIMISE THE SPACE OF YOUR APPLIANCE (SEE TIP). DEHYDRATE ONE TYPE OF FRUIT AT A TIME.

DRIED WATERMELON

800g wedge of seedless watermelon

DRIED PINEAPPLE

1 medium pineapple (1.2kg)

DRIED APPLE

2 medium red-skinned apples (450g)

DRIED KIWIFRUIT

4 medium kiwifruit (340g)

DRIED WATERMELON Using a sharp knife, cut watermelon into 2–3mm-thick slices.

DRIED PINEAPPLE Using a sharp knife, cut pineapple in half crossways through the middle (reserve other half for another use). Peel then remove the core with an apple corer. Thinly slice pineapple into 2mm-thick rings.

DRIED APPLE Using a mandoline or V-slicer, thinly slice apples into 1–2mm-thick slices.

DRIED KIWIFRUIT Peel kiwifruit, then thinly slice into 2mm-thick slices.

1 For all fruit, lightly spray a 5-tier dehydrator rack with olive oil cooking spray.

2 Arrange either watermelon, pineapple, apple or kiwifruit slices in a single layer on the rack tiers, then place rack in the inner pot. Cover with the air fryer lid. Select **DEHYDRATE** and set temperature to 70°C and time for 4 hours; **DEHYDRATE** until fruit is dried.

3 Remove the dehydrator rack from the inner pot. Leave fruit to cool on the rack. Store in an airtight container for up to 2 weeks.

TIP If you do not have a 5-tier dehydrator rack, halve the recipe and place half the fruit in a single layer in the air fryer basket, cover with the perforated tray, then place remaining fruit on top. Place the air fryer basket in the inner pot and continue with the recipe.

BAKE

KEEP THE KITCHEN COOL AND USE YOUR INSTANT POT® INSTEAD OF THE OVEN

BAKE UP A SPREAD OF CAKES, PIES, ROLLS AND BREADS.

PREP
25 MINS

BAKE
2 HRS 30 MINS

SERVES
4

POTATO & FRENCH ONION BAKE

- 1.2kg desiree potatoes, peeled, cut into 5mm-thick slices
- 2 tbsp lemon thyme leaves
- 40g packet French onion soup mix
- 300ml thickened cream
- ¼ cup (60ml) milk
- ½ cup (40g) finely grated vegetarian parmesan-style cheese

TO SERVE
- extra lemon thyme leaves

1 Lightly grease a 20cm round cake pan. Arrange potatoes upright in stacks of slices around the edge of the pan, then work towards the centre to completely cover the base of the pan, scattering with thyme as you go.

2 Combine soup mix, cream, milk and parmesan in a large jug; season with salt and pepper. Pour mixture evenly over the potatoes and let it settle. Cover the pan with foil. Place pan in the inner pot. Cover with the air fryer lid. Select **BAKE** and set temperature to 180°C and time for 2 hours.

3 Remove the foil, then re-cover with the air fryer lid. Select **BAKE** and set temperature to 200°C and time for 30 minutes; **BAKE** until potato is tender and top is golden.

4 Stand bake for 10 minutes before serving. Serve topped with extra thyme leaves.

TIP Fold two lengths of foil into long strips and cross under base of pan to act as a sling; this will make it easier to lower and lift the pan into and out of the inner pot.

PREP
30 MINS (+ STANDING)

BAKE
30 MINS

MAKES
9

CHELSEA BUNS

¾ cup (180ml) milk, heated to lukewarm

¼ cup firmly packed (55g) brown sugar

2 tsp (7g) dried yeast

50g butter, melted, cooled

3 cups (480g) bread flour

1½ tsp mixed spice

1 egg, beaten lightly

25g butter, extra, softened

¾ cup (100g) craisins, chopped coarsely

½ cup (80g) icing sugar

3 tsp milk, extra, approx.

1 Combine lukewarm milk, 1 tbsp brown sugar and the yeast in a medium bowl. Stand in a warm place for 10 minutes or until mixture is frothy. Stir in melted butter.

2 Place flour and ½ tsp mixed spice in the large bowl of an electric mixer fitted with a dough hook. Add yeast mixture and egg; mix for 10 minutes or until a smooth and elastic dough forms. Transfer dough to a large oiled bowl and cover with plastic wrap. Stand in a warm place for 1 hour or until doubled in size.

3 Grease and line base and side of a 20cm round cake pan. Punch dough down with a fist, then turn out onto a lightly floured surface. Knead dough until smooth, then roll into a 25cm x 42cm rectangle. Spread extra butter over dough; scatter with craisins and sprinkle with combined remaining mixed spice and brown sugar. Roll dough up firmly from a long side and trim ends; cut into nine equal slices. Place eight scrolls, cut-side up and just touching, around the edge of the pan and one in the centre. Cover and stand in a warm place for 30 minutes or until risen.

4 Place the wire rack in the inner pot, then place the pan on top. Cover with the air fryer lid. Select **BAKE** and set temperature to 160°C and time for 30 minutes; **BAKE** until buns are golden brown.

5 Meanwhile, to make the icing, sift icing sugar into a small bowl; stir in enough milk to form a thin, smooth paste.

6 Carefully remove pan from the inner pot. Turn buns out onto a wire rack and drizzle with icing. Cool.

TIP You can also use the appliance to prove the dough in steps 2 and 3. To do this, place a folded tea towel in the base of the inner pot, then place the bowl/cake pan on top. Select **WARM** and set time for the specified time.

GOOD TO
FREEZE

PREP	SAUTÉ	BAKE	SERVES
10 MINS	10 MINS	40 MINS	4

MEATBALLS WITH MOZZARELLA & RISONI

2 medium red onions (340g)

2 tbsp extra virgin olive oil

4 cloves garlic, crushed

2 x 400g cans diced tomatoes

2 tbsp tomato paste

1½ cups (375ml) beef stock

1 tbsp brown sugar

1 tbsp balsamic vinegar

1 cup (220g) risoni

⅓ cup (55g) pitted Sicilian green olives, torn

MEATBALLS

1 bunch fresh oregano

500g pork and veal mince

50g firm mozzarella, grated

50g finely grated parmesan

1 egg

1 cup (70g) stale breadcrumbs

1¼ tsp sea salt flakes

1 Coarsely grate half an onion. Thinly slice remaining onions.

2 To make the meatballs, chop oregano and combine with grated onion, the mince, mozzarella, 25g parmesan, egg, breadcrumbs and salt; season with pepper. Using your hands, combine mixture very well. Shape ¼ cups of mixture into balls and place on a tray. Cover and refrigerate until required.

3 Select **SAUTÉ** high heat and preheat for 8 minutes. When the inner pot is hot, add oil, then add the meatballs; **SAUTÉ**, turning, for 2 minutes or until meatballs are browned. Transfer meatballs to a tray.

4 Add sliced onion to the inner pot and **SAUTÉ** for 5 minutes or until soft and golden. Add garlic and **SAUTÉ**, stirring, for a further 1 minute or until fragrant. Add tomatoes, tomato paste, stock, sugar and vinegar, then season well with salt and pepper; bring to the boil. Add the meatballs.

5 Cover with the air fryer lid. Select **BAKE** and set temperature to 180°C and time for 30 minutes.

6 Add risoni and olives to the inner pot; stir gently to combine. Re-cover with the air fryer lid. Select **BAKE** and set temperature to 180°C and time for 10 minutes; **BAKE** until risoni is tender.

7 Serve meatballs and risoni sprinkled with remaining parmesan.

PREP	BAKE	SAUTÉ	SERVES
15 MINS	1 HR 30 MINS	5 MINS	8

BANANA CAKE WITH CREAM CHEESE FROSTING & MISO CARAMEL

150g unsalted butter, melted

½ cup (110g) firmly packed dark brown sugar

¼ cup (90g) golden syrup

¼ cup (60g) white (shiro) miso

2 eggs

1 cup (280g) mashed ripe banana

1½ cups (225g) self-raising flour

½ cup (75g) plain flour

1½ tsp ground cinnamon

½ cup (55g) coarsely chopped walnuts

½ cup (125ml) buttermilk

MISO CARAMEL

1 cup (350g) honey

1 cup (250ml) pouring cream

1½ tbsp white (shiro) miso

CREAM CHEESE FROSTING

375g cream cheese

½ cup (80g) icing sugar mixture

1 Grease an 18cm round cake pan; line base and side with baking paper.

2 Whisk butter, sugar, golden syrup, miso and eggs in a medium bowl until well combined; stir in banana. Fold in combined sifted flours and cinnamon, walnuts and buttermilk until well combined. Pour mixture into pan and smooth the surface. Cover loosely with foil.

3 Place the air fryer base in the inner pot, then place the pan on top. Cover with the air fryer lid. Select **BAKE** and set temperature to 180°C and time for 1 hour 10 minutes.

4 Remove the foil, then re-cover with the air fryer lid. Select **BAKE** and set temperature to 180°C and time for 20 minutes; **BAKE** until a skewer inserted in the centre comes out clean.

5 Remove the pan from the inner pot. Leave cake in pan for 10 minutes before turning top-side up onto a wire rack to cool completely.

6 Meanwhile, to make the miso caramel, select **SAUTÉ** high heat. Add honey to the inner pot; **SAUTÉ** for 3 minutes or until darkened. Taking care, as mixture will splatter, stir in cream then miso until smooth. Cool to room temperature.

7 To make the cream cheese frosting, process ingredients until smooth. Refrigerate until required.

8 Spread top of cake with cream cheese frosting, then drizzle with miso caramel.

DAIRY FREE
GOOD TO FREEZE

PREP	SAUTÉ	BAKE	SERVES
15 MINS	16 MINS	20 MINS	4

HAM HOCK, CHICKEN & LEEK PIE

800g chicken thigh fillets, sliced thinly

2 tbsp olive oil

1 large leek (500g), sliced thinly

2 cloves garlic, crushed

1 tbsp thyme leaves

¼ cup (35g) plain flour

3 cups (750ml) chicken stock

600g ham hock, meat removed, shredded

2 sheets puff pastry, thawed (see tips)

1 egg, beaten lightly

TO SERVE
extra thyme sprigs

1 Select **SAUTÉ** high heat and preheat for 5 minutes. Season chicken. When the inner pot is hot, add half the oil, then add half the chicken; **SAUTÉ**, stirring occasionally, for 3 minutes or until browned. Transfer chicken to a plate. Repeat with remaining oil and chicken; transfer to plate.

2 Add leek to the inner pot and **SAUTÉ**, stirring occasionally, for 3 minutes or until softened. Add garlic and thyme; **SAUTÉ** for a further 1 minute or until fragrant. Return the chicken to the inner pot with flour; **SAUTÉ**, stirring, for 1 minute. Gradually stir in stock and bring to the boil; **SAUTÉ**, stirring continuously, for a further 5 minutes or until thickened slightly. Stir in ham and season. Check a deep 20cm pie tin fits in the inner pot, then transfer filling to the tin. Wipe the inner pot clean and return to the appliance. Place the wire rack in the pot.

3 Trim pastry to fit the top of the tin, then brush with egg. Place tin on the wire rack in the inner pot. Cover with the air fryer lid. Select **BAKE** and set temperature to 200°C and time for 20 minutes; **BAKE** until pastry is golden.

4 Serve pie scattered with extra thyme sprigs.

TIPS For a dairy-free diet, ensure you purchase regular puff pastry which is dairy free, and not butter puff pastry which contains butter. The filling can be made up to 2 days ahead; cover and keep refrigerated. The baked pie can be frozen for up to 3 months.

PREP 10 MINS | BAKE 40 MINS | SERVES 4

APPLE & BERRY GINGER CRUMBLES

FILLING

4 medium pink lady apples (600g), cut into 1.5cm-thick slices

750g dark berries (if using cherries, halve and pit) (see tip)

200g seedless red grapes, halved

¼ cup (35g) plain flour

⅓ cup (75g) caster sugar

1 tsp vanilla bean paste

1 tsp ground ginger

CRUMBLE

1 cup (130g) crispy oat clusters chunky nut

¼ cup (30g) almond meal

40g butter, melted

½ tsp ground ginger

1 tbsp honey

½ cup (80g) natural almonds, roasted, chopped coarsely

¼ cup (55g) coarsely chopped crystallised ginger

TO SERVE

custard

1 To make the filling, place ingredients in a large bowl; toss until fruit is well combined and coated in flour and sugar.

2 To make the crumble, combine ingredients in a medium bowl. Using your fingertips, press the mixture into clumps.

3 Place the air fryer base in the inner pot. Grease four 1½-cup ovenproof dishes (or a large round 1.75-litre/7-cup ovenproof dish). Check the dishes fit in the inner pot.

4 Spoon filling into the dishes and top with crumble; loosely cover with foil. Place the dishes in the inner pot. Cover with the air fryer lid. Select **BAKE** and set temperature to 180°C and time for 30 minutes.

5 Remove the foil, then re-cover with the air fryer lid. Select **BAKE** and set temperature to 180°C and time for 10 minutes; **BAKE** until fruit is tender and crumble is golden.

6 Serve crumbles warm, drizzled with custard.

TIP For dark berries, use a mix of fresh or frozen cherries, blackberries and blueberries, or only one type.

TIP You can also use the appliance to prove the dough in steps 2 and 3. To do this, place a folded tea towel in the base of the inner pot, then place the bowl/cake pan on top. Select **WARM** and set time for the specified time.

PREP	BAKE	SERVES
15 MINS (+ STANDING)	1 HR	8

NO-KNEAD UKRAINIAN DINNER ROLLS (PAMPUSHKY)

- 2 tsp (7g) dried yeast
- ¼ cup (55g) caster sugar
- ½ cup (125ml) warm water
- 3¾ cups (600g) bread flour, plus extra for dusting
- 2 tsp fine sea salt
- 2 eggs, beaten lightly
- 90g butter, melted
- ¾ cup (180ml) milk, approx.
- 1 egg yolk, beaten with 2 tsp water
- 1 clove garlic, crushed
- ¼ cup coarsely chopped flat-leaf parsley

1 Whisk yeast, 1 tbsp sugar and the water in a medium jug until dissolved. Stand for 10 minutes or until mixture is frothy.

2 Place flour, salt and remaining sugar in a large bowl, then make a well in the centre. Pour in yeast mixture, beaten egg and 50g butter; stir in enough milk to form a soft, slightly sticky dough. Cover with a clean, damp tea towel. Stand in a warm place for 45 minutes or until doubled in size.

3 Punch dough down with a fist; turn out onto a lightly floured surface. Fold over several times until smooth. Divide into eight equal portions, then roll into balls. Grease a 22cm round cake pan. Place seven dough balls around the edge of the pan and one in the centre. Cover with a damp tea towel. Stand in a warm place for 20 minutes or until nearly doubled in size.

4 Meanwhile, place the air fryer basket in the inner pot. Cover with the air fryer lid. Select **BAKE** and set temperature to 200°C and time for 8 minutes to preheat.

5 Brush the rolls with egg wash. Place pan in the inner pot. Cover with the air fryer lid. Select **BAKE** and set temperature to 180°C and time for 10 minutes.

6 Cover rolls with foil, then re-cover with the air fryer lid. Select **BAKE** and set temperature to 180°C and time for 50 minutes; **BAKE** until rolls sound hollow when tapped. Leave in pan for 5 minutes before transferring to a wire rack.

7 Combine garlic, parsley and remaining butter in a small bowl. Brush warm rolls with garlic butter and serve warm.

PREP	SAUTÉ	BAKE	SERVES
10 MINS	7 MINS	15 MINS	4

MEXICAN MAC & CHEESE

400g macaroni

60g butter, chopped

60g plain flour

3 cups (750ml) milk

¼ cup (65g) chipotle in adobo sauce, chopped

200g Mexican shredded cheese

2 trimmed corn cobs (500g), kernels removed

3 green onions, sliced thinly

100g corn chips, crushed

TO SERVE
hot sauce and chopped coriander leaves

1 Bring a saucepan of salted water to the boil. Cook macaroni for 2 minutes, then drain well. (The macaroni will only be partially cooked at this stage.)

2 Meanwhile, select **SAUTÉ** high heat and preheat for 5 minutes. When the inner pot is hot, add butter. Once butter is melted, add flour; **SAUTÉ**, stirring for 1 minute or until a sandy texture. Gradually add milk, stirring until smooth and well combined for 3 minutes. Add chipotle and half the cheese; **SAUTÉ**, stirring, for 2 minutes until cheese is melted. Stir in half the green onion and macaroni; season. Scatter with remaining cheese.

3 Cover with the air fryer lid. Select **BAKE** and set temperature to 180°C and time for 15 minutes; **BAKE** until top is golden.

4 Serve mac and cheese topped with corn chips, hot sauce, coriander leaves and remaining green onion.

GOOD TO FREEZE
VEGETARIAN

PREP	DEHYDRATE	BAKE	SERVES
15 MINS	4 HRS	1 HR 35 MINS	6–8

PINK GRAPEFRUIT & POPPYSEED POUND CAKE

2 small ruby red grapefruit (700g)

250g butter, softened

1 cup (220g) caster sugar

1½ tbsp poppy seeds

4 eggs

½ cup (75g) self-raising flour, sifted

1 cup (150g) plain flour, sifted

1¾ cups (280g) icing sugar, sifted

1 Thinly slice 1 grapefruit. Place the air fryer basket in the inner pot. Place half the slices over the base of the basket, then place the perforated tray on top. Place remaining slices on the tray. Cover with the air fryer lid. Select **DEHYDRATE** and set temperature to 70°C and time for 4 hours. Transfer slices to a plate to cool.

2 Grease a deep 18cm round cake pan; line base with baking paper. Cover with the air fryer lid. Select **BAKE** and set temperature to 180°C and time for 10 minutes to preheat.

3 Finely grate the rind from remaining grapefruit, then juice; you need 2 tbsp rind and ¼ cup (60ml) juice. Beat butter, caster sugar, grapefruit rind and poppy seeds in a large bowl with an electric mixer until light and fluffy. Beat in eggs one at a time. Fold in combined flours in two batches. Spread mixture in pan and cover tightly with foil.

4 Place the air fryer base in the inner pot, then place the pan on top. Cover with the air fryer lid. Select **BAKE** and set temperature to 180°C and time for 1 hour 15 minutes.

5 Remove the foil, then re-cover with the air fryer lid. Select **BAKE** and set temperature to 180°C and time for 20 minutes; **BAKE** until a skewer inserted in the centre comes out clean. Remove the pan from the inner pot. Leave cake in pan for 10 minutes before turning top-side up onto a wire rack to cool completely.

6 To make the icing, whisk icing sugar and grapefruit juice in a small bowl until smooth. Spread icing over cake, then top with dehydrated grapefruit slices.

CONVERSION CHART

MEASURES

One Australian metric measuring cup holds approximately 250ml; one Australian metric tablespoon holds 20ml; one Australian metric teaspoon holds 5ml. North America, New Zealand and the United Kingdom use a 15ml tablespoon.

The difference between one country's measuring cups and another's is within a two- or three-teaspoon variance and will not affect your cooking results. All cup and spoon measurements are level.

The most accurate way of measuring dry ingredients is to weigh them.

When measuring liquids, use a clear glass or plastic jug with metric markings.

We use extra-large eggs with an average weight of 60g each.

DRY MEASURES

metric	imperial
15g	½oz
30g	1oz
60g	2oz
90g	3oz
125g	4oz (¼lb)
155g	5oz
185g	6oz
220g	7oz
250g	8oz (½lb)
280g	9oz
315g	10oz
345g	11oz
375g	12oz (¾lb)
410g	13oz
440g	14oz
470g	15oz
500g	16oz (1lb)
750g	24oz (1½lb)
1kg	32oz (2lb)

LIQUID MEASURES

metric	imperial
30ml	1 fluid oz
60ml	2 fluid oz
100ml	3 fluid oz
125ml	4 fluid oz
150ml	5 fluid oz
190ml	6 fluid oz
250ml	8 fluid oz
300ml	10 fluid oz
500ml	16 fluid oz
600ml	20 fluid oz
1000ml (1 litre)	1¾ pints

LENGTH MEASURES

metric	imperial
3mm	⅛in
6mm	¼in
1cm	½in
2cm	¾in
2.5cm	1in
5cm	2in
6cm	2½in
8cm	3in
10cm	4in
13cm	5in
15cm	6in
18cm	7in
20cm	8in
22cm	9in
25cm	10in
28cm	11in
30cm	12in (1ft)

OVEN TEMPERATURES

The oven temperatures below are for conventional ovens; if you are using a fan-forced oven, reduce the temperature by 20 degrees.

	°C (Celsius)	°F (Fahrenheit)
Very slow	120	250
Slow	150	300
Moderately slow	160	325
Moderate	180	350
Moderately hot	200	400
Hot	220	425
Very hot	240	475

Measurements for cake pans are approximate only. Using same-shaped cake pans of a similar size should not affect the outcome of your baking. We measure the inside top of the cake pan to determine size.

INDEX

R

S

T

V

W

Z

PUBLISHED IN 2023 BY ARE MEDIA BOOKS, AUSTRALIA.
ARE MEDIA BOOKS IS A DIVISION OF ARE MEDIA PTY LIMITED.

ARE MEDIA

Chief Executive Officer Jane Huxley

ARE MEDIA BOOKS

Group Publisher Nicole Byers
Editorial & Food Director Sophia Young
Books Director David Scotto
Creative Director Hannah Blackmore
Managing Editor Stephanie Kistner
Senior Designer Kelsie Walker
Food Editor Sophia Young
Senior Editor Chantal Gibbs

Photographer Con Poulos
Stylist Olivia Blackmore
Photochefs Rebecca Lyall, Clare Maguire

 womensweeklyfood

 @womensweeklyfood

TRUSTED BRANDS USED IN OUR TEST KITCHEN

Printed in China by
Leo Paper Products

A catalogue record for this book is available from the National Library of Australia.
ISBN 978-1-76122-065-4 (paperback)

ABN 18 053 273 546

Published by Are Media Books, a division of Are Media Pty Limited, 54 Park St, Sydney; GPO Box 4088, Sydney, NSW 2001, Australia
Ph +61 2 9282 8000

www.awwcookbooks.com.au

INSTANT POT® is a registered trade mark of Instant Brands Inc.

International rights enquiries
internationalrights@aremedia.com.au

Order Books
Phone 1300 322 007 (within Australia)

Or order online at
www.awwcookbooks.com.au

Send recipe enquiries to
recipeenquiries@aremedia.com.au